My Inner Child Must Be Heard

My Inner Child Must Be Heard

From Despair to Dancing on the Clouds

Corina Zalace

Copyright © 2014 by Corina Zalace.

Library of Congress Control Number: 2014911208
ISBN: Hardcover   978-1-4990-3929-0
           Softcover   978-1-4990-3930-6
           eBook   978-1-4990-3928-3

All rights reserved. No part of this book may be reproduced or transmitted in any form or by any means, electronic or mechanical, including photocopying, recording, or by any information storage and retrieval system, without permission in writing from the copyright owner.

Any people depicted in stock imagery provided by Thinkstock are models, and such images are being used for illustrative purposes only.
Certain stock imagery © Thinkstock.

Scriptures and additional materials quoted are from the Good News Bible © 1994 published by the Bible Societies/HarperCollins Publishers Ltd UK, Good News Bible© American Bible Society 1966, 1971, 1976, 1992. Used with permission.

This book was printed in the United States of America.

Rev. date: 06/24/2014

To order additional copies of this book, contact:
Xlibris LLC
1-888-795-4274
www.Xlibris.com
Orders@Xlibris.com
540935

Contents

Preface 7
Mom 9
Prologue 13

Polio 17
My Handicap 19
My Bulemia Struggle 21
Defenses 25
The Volcano 29
Denial 33
The Abyss 35
My Battle With Control 39
Pit Of Depression 43
Depression Deep 47
Owning My Feelings 49
My Many Faces 53
False Masks 57
Anger 61
My Wall Of Shame 65
The Games We Play 67
Part One: Preface 71
Part Two: The River 72
Part Three: My Handicap 75
Part Four: My Hiding Place 79
Part Five: The Secret 84
Part Six: The Silence 87
Part Seven: Who Am I? 89
Part Eight: My Left Over Pain 96
My Heart's Cry 101
Pain And Purpose 105

My Purpose In Life	107
Old Messages--New Messages	110
From Down To Up!	113
Grace	118
Hospital Nights	121
My Gift	123
Letting Go	125
My Pain	129
Abba Father	131
My Vow	133
Will You Still Stand?	136
God Is Still There	139
God's Incredible Joy	141
My Prayer--Psalm 63	143
Psalm 91:1	144
The Darkness	146
Choices	149
When You Feel . . .	151
If Only . . .	160
Habakkuk 3: 17 – 18	162
The Transformation	165
Healing From My Secret	167
Epilogue	173
Postscript	175
No Man Is An Island	176

Preface

Why my Mom?

I question everything. Why this, why that, why not? I have always had a real problem, because I analyze anything I'm told, wondering what was "really" meant by a statement. All this questioning and wondering has caused me many problems. One of my biggest struggles has to do with the fact that my mother is in a wheelchair, having had polio when she was two. Ever since I was a little girl, my mom has been "different" from other moms. She can't run, she can't dance, she can barely walk a dozen steps.

In my childhood innocence I believed it just wasn't fair. How could God be so cruel to my mother? Why my mom? Sometimes I even prayed that we could switch places, and that I would wake up with her paralysis. That way, she could enjoy the simple pleasures in life such as taking a walk, strolling on the beach, or running through a meadow, which we all take for granted. I have always been taught that everything happens for a purpose. No matter how hard I tried, I could not see why my mom had to be handicapped. I couldn't understand it. I prayed to God, asking Him to please heal my mommy, to please take away her pain, to please dry her unshed tears.

My mother, on the other hand, had no doubt that God was going to heal her, and still stands strong in that conviction. In the Bible, Hebrews 11, verse 1 says "Now faith is the assurance of things hoped for, the conviction of things not seen." She lives by this verse, knowing that her faith will prevail. She has accepted her handicap as a part of life and works to make the best of her situation. She leaves a lasting impression on the life of everyone she touches. How can you complain about how unfair or hard life is, faced with a woman who is confined to a wheelchair, yet who takes everything in stride? My mom has a smile for everyone, and although in constant pain, she is rarely down. In fact, she lifts all those around her up. This is a cold slap of humility for me everytime I start to complain, because at that moment she always seems to enter the room with her contented smile.

All of this had never stopped my questioning: Why my mom? What purpose does her handicap serve? Then, slowly, God began to reveal it to me through other people. My mother is a witness for the Lord. It means so much to hear my mom talk about her faith and love for God. Anyone can proclaim their faith, but here is a vibrant woman, confined to a wheelchair, who is content with her life and thanks God every day for her many blessings. This touches others as no ordinary witness could, because it also gives them that same cold slap of humility. What right do they have to be discontented with God, when she is so content? My mother has touched so many lives in a way that she could have never done if she were not handicapped.

Over the years, God has taught me a valuable lesson by letting me understand Romans 8, verse 28, as it applies to my mother's life: "We know that all things work together for good for those who love God." My Lord has shown me that everything does happen for a purpose, you just have to wait on Him to find out what that purpose is.

God is teaching me to wait on His time through my mother. I have written her this poem to show that I am beginning to understand and truly appreciate the gift that God has given her.

Mom

I wonder if you know
Just how much you mean to me?
My love that overflows
I wonder if you can see?
Do you know the pain my heart hides,
Every time I see you cry?
Can you sense my hidden hurt
Every time I hear you sigh?
You've always comforted me
Whenever I've gotten hurt,
Patched up every scratch
And wiped away all the dirt.
Even when I don't listen,
And turn your advice aside,
I always know you love me
And will stick right by my side.
You seem able to erase all my pain,
I wish I could do the same for you.
I want to stop your hurt and suffering,
The anguish that you go through.
But we both know this isn't God's will,
It isn't what He has in mind.
We have to wait for His timing,
When all his mysteries He'll unwind.
So I have to believe everything happens for a purpose,
We just don't know what God has in store.
But one of these days He'll hand you the key
And you'll be able to *walk* through that door!

Giselle Washburn

Thanks To:

God for being my Healer, Savior, Comforter, and the Lord of my life. He continues to set me free.

My husband Stan who not only unfailingly stood by my side as I went through the difficult times in my life, but also spent the time necessary to edit this book.

My children who believed in me and wanted nothing more than for me to be set free from my inner demons.

My mother who instilled in me that I was a survivor, gave me a never give up attitude, and always told me that there was nothing I could not do.

My dad who stood faithfully by my side through each childhood surgery I had, and who gave me the reassuring image of his never failing strength by my side.

My siblings Marge, Nicky and Pete who have always stood by my side and encouraged me with this project.

My dear friends who showered me with prayer and encouragement.

Corina Zalace

"I must have a solid foundation of belief in all things true about God upon which my grief and tears can fall, otherwise my tears will create a pool in which I will eventually drown."

Nicolet Timmer

Prologue

"WHAT?!!! You are putting me on the mental ward?!!! NO!!! I went ballistic. "I DON'T BELONG THERE. MY MIND IS FINE. I DON'T BELONG IN THE "LOONEY TUNE WARD!!!" My mind was racing as I tried to figure out something I could say to convince my therapist and my husband that I was not crazy and was really fine. OK, so I had just said I wanted to die, wanted to go home and just take a bunch of pills, and if I didn't wake up the next morning that was fine with me. But really... was that a reason to put me in a locked mental ward?! Every emotion I had ever felt exploded through my brain. I pleaded, I cried, I screamed out in fury. I was scared to death, but to no avail as my husband Stan continued driving me to the hospital. I told him I'd be good and do whatever he and my therapist would tell me to do. His response was "This will be for your own good and to protect you Princess." That was his pet name for me, Princess, but I did not feel like a princess as he drove me to what I was sure was my doom.

PROTECT ME FROM WHAT?!!! More pleading and begging to just take me home. Stan would not relent. I felt like I was being punished for doing something really bad. Whatever I could think of, I said to try to convince my husband that yes, my body had been screwed up by polio since I was 2 years old, but my mind was fine. I was proud of that. And now my mind seemed to be messed up, too. NO...I could not handle that at all! The polio had robbed me of a full life and deceived me, and now my mind? Everything inside of me felt wrong. But Stan was unmoved and continued driving me to the hospital. By then I really did feel like dying. My own husband had apparently turned my therapist against me.

Instead of being taken to the civilian hospital so my own psychiatrist and therapist—people I knew--could see me, I was taken to the nearby military hospital since my husband was in the military. I dreaded going to a military hospital and being seen by some new doctor and therapists who had no clue who I was. I was seething!!! By the time we got to the hospital, I had decided that I would raise hell for the military staff and doctor and make it clear that I did not want to be there. AND I DID!!! I refused to eat in the patient dining area. I'd starve before I'd get out of bed to do what they said. One airman had compassion on me and delivered a food tray to my room. Every morning when I saw the psychiatrist, I made it very clear that I did not want to be there and became completely uncooperative and obnoxious. I created such an uproar for him that he gladly released me on the third day and sent me to the civilian hospital. Now I had MY psychiatrist and therapist, people who knew me, to work with me. That felt better. But I was still a prisoner.

Yet it was so unlike me to act this hateful way. I was always cooperative and sweet and everyone liked me. I had no enemies and tried to please those around me. Now here I was with this monster inside of me trying to get out. What was happening to me? And the strangest thing is that I did not care what anyone thought. I used to always care what others thought. I'd go to great lengths to be there for everyone, and to be nice to them. To live up to a shining image I had crafted for myself. But now it was different. Sitting on my bed right after being readmitted, I had my first meal, a food tray sitting in front of me in my room. I took the plastic knife that came with the meal and began cutting on my left wrist. At that moment a part of me split off. It was as if I was standing on the side of my bed, watching myself cutting my wrist. My mind recoiled, and in a panic I said to myself "Maybe I really am crazy and really do belong here".

My mind raced back to my childhood. I had developed a severe eating disorder when I was 14 years old, and had no idea why. All I could sense at the time was that I was sinking deeper and deeper into a shadowy pit of depression, and no one seemed to care. I didn't know how to deal with the pain inside me safely, how to let it out without hurting others. I thought all I was doing was sinning and I felt only deep shame, guilt, and that I was a phony. And as an adult, I still did not understand, and things just got worse. Here I was, a church going woman who loved God as much as I could love Him, was on the church praise team leading people into worship every Sunday morning, led worship at Bible Study groups with my guitar, and yet at the same time lived this secret shameful life on the side. I was consumed by guilt!!! Every song I sang became a desperate prayer, as deep inside my breaking heart cried out to God. My life became a prayer of desperation to Him. I truly was a Godly mess! And I had no clue how to end the chaos my life had become. I thought of suicide often, but was too scared to follow through. All of these thoughts racing through my mind, my life became impossible on the mental ward. And I had no clue that what was to happen to me over the next 17 plus years would be the most painful, yet the most freeing period of my life. Or so I thought. For the 33 years I had hurt so badly inside that I did not understand why I had sunk into such a deep depression, and why I would hurt myself for relief. And now I had to put the pieces together if I ever hoped to enjoy a "normal" life.

So one day I decided to open up to a nurse who was a patient also. She was in the mental ward for severe depression. I showed her my, by then, oozing wound from cutting on myself with the plastic knife. I asked her "Why did I do that?" Her response was that the pain inside of me was so great, but couldn't be seen, that I had to physically see it somehow to know and see that I was still alive. Then everything began to make sense to me; about my childhood years, when I would deliberately hurt myself to the point of causing bruising. Yet my family never noticed. How could I let them know how much I was hurting inside? I made the bruises so obvious, but no one asked about them, and so I kept my inner pain a secret buried deep within me. I could not find the voice I needed to tell anyone of my suffering. And all I was ever told anyway by my mother was how strong and brave I always was, especially when my dad and I would pull out of the driveway in our station wagon on yet another long drive through the early morning Los Angeles traffic to the hospital for another one of the many surgeries on my legs. So how could I let her down when she counted on me to be her "strong and brave little Corina."

This book is a collection of poems and artwork created over the years after I realized I had a problem and got help. They trace how God set me free of all the shame, guilt and pain I struggled with from my traumatic childhood and adulthood. Besides the polio which has now confined me to a wheelchair, I have suffered from an eating disorder most of my life, was sexually molested and raped as a child by adult caregivers outside my family, have had over 90 major and minor surgeries, suffered depression most of my life, abused myself in various ways to numb out my pain, had breast cancer, and today suffer from chronic pain. In spite of all this, today I can truthfully say that God has set me free emotionally and filled me with His joy, which is my strength. It is my deepest desire that my poetry can help others who are burdened by depression, guilt, shame and pain from their personal traumas. May God bless you.

Corina Zalace

Polio

When I as a child was paralyzed,
I cried out in fear and pain.
From the polio that struck me,
Terror filled my every vein.

Sapped of all energy and strength,
Frail I soon became.
Trapped within a body
That made me ache with shame.

I did not understand
What was going on.
I was so little
And just wanted my mom.

Even she could not
Take all the pain away.
The vomiting, the fever,
The hot and cold sweats all stayed.

The pain of spasms
That ran through me;
Every limb was affected
Yet no comfort could there be.

My legs limp,
I could not even stand.
But with much therapy
I regained some use in the end.

Many surgeries
I had to endure--
To help me become
Independent and sure.

I have so many scars
From the battles I have waged;
And still my strength declined,
As the disease endlessly raged.

I used one crutch for years,
Then finally two;
And at last a leg brace
Was even added, too.

Now I'm in a wheelchair,
But it has not held me back,
For I keep on surviving
And daily challenges attack.

Soldiering for Jesus
For in His army I fight;
He's my Commander
And He'll lead me aright.

My Handicap

I grew up feeling
Odd and out of place,
Not fitting in
Any of life's normal ways.

Stares of many people
I came to despise;
Ridicule and taunting
Crushed me like a vise.

Feeling mocking eyes upon me
Like a freak on display,
My handicap kept me limping
Every step of every day.

The pain of rejection
Was too much to bear.
I just could not handle
Everyone's piercing stare.

So I built a wall
High and thick in me;
And I hid behind it
So no one could see.

See my incredible pain
And deep rooted shame
For how I was treated,
Yet I took all the blame.

The blame for my handicap,
Not accepting how I am.
Because of all the ridicule,
My wall became a dam.

All feelings locked up,
Including my deep pain.
Yet I did not feel safe
And still felt so much shame.

Then God opened my eyes
To see that my wall
Was a wall of shame
That only kept building tall.

It kept me from receiving
The love and healings
I so badly needed
To let go of all my feelings.

My Bulemia Struggle

Torment boils
In my mind;
Confusion and chaos
Is all I find.

Negative thoughts
Never let up;
Negative emotions
Constantly erupt.

No rest I find
Amidst this war
That is waging
Non-stop so far.

The enemy
Of my soul,
Is keeping me
In this dark hole.

"I'll never heal",
One of my fears;
Hopelessness,
Through me sears.

How do I stop
These negative voices
Bombarding me?
What are my choices?

For this torment
Consumes me;
I cannot see
My way free.

For I feel trapped
As in a hell;
My body becomes
An emaciated shell.

Yet fat
Is all I feel.
And often I don't
Know what is real.

Affirmations
I must choose,
To help me through
This enemy's abuse.

But no matter
How hard I try,
I can't do it
Alone and get by.

Those who love me,
Do they care?
Are they safe?
Can I share?

I need help
From my friends,
So I can receive
The love God sends.

*God, please don't
Give up on me.
My deepest desire
Is to be free.*

How long will
This torment last?
Most of my life
Has already past.

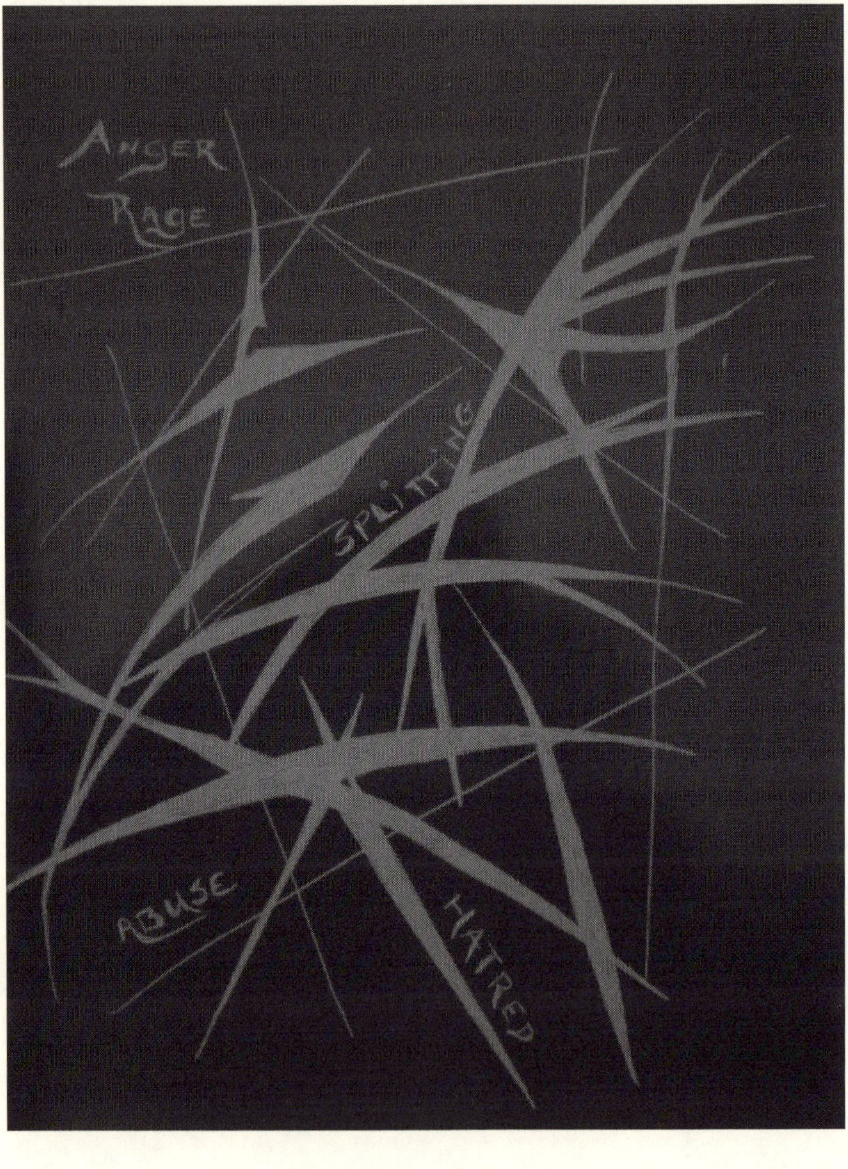
ANGER
RAGE
SPLITTING
ABUSE
HATRED

Defenses

Comfortably I sit
In my protected room
That I have built
To hide in, like a womb.

My negative emotions
And my past hurts,
Surround me here
And come at me in spurts.

Running from the pain
That others inflict on me,
I lock myself tightly
In walls that surround me.

Feeling safe inside,
No one can come near.
But soon I realize
My prison is my fear.

Fear of being hurt.
Fear of opening up.
Fear of letting others
See my emotions erupt.

My four thick walls
Not only hold my fear,
They also lock out
All the love that is near.

For only true love
Can heal me from within.
So I must decide
How to let it in.

A key to the one door
Of my prison cell I hold.
I only can open it
And take this step so bold.

So I unlock the door
To let true love in,
To bring real healing
To all my pain within.

As love permeates
The corners of my room,
It heals and replaces
My hurts and fears of doom.

Then I discover
That deep inside
Is the real me
That for years I did hide..

Like an adventure
I am discovering
Who I really am
As I am recovering.

OUT OF CONTROL!
ALL EMOTIONS
BAD DAY!

The Volcano

The mountain looks
Peaceful as can be.
Beautiful vegetation
And wild flowers I see.

Trees are everywhere,
And birds are flitting
Through the picture perfect scene,
And butterflies are fluttering.

The beauty all around
Inspires me with awe,
For all I can see
Is nature with no flaw.

Yet very deep down
In the mountain's core,
Pressure is threatening
As never before

This mountain really is
A volcano, you see;
Full of molten lava
Pushing to be free.

From the outside
There is only peace,
But on the inside,
Turmoil that won't cease.

I am like that mountain,
Cloaked in peace, serene.
No one sees that inside
It is a most chaotic scene.

There are feelings deep,
I never knew were there.
They were hidden deep
So others I would not scare.

Just as the lava inside
Boils up from the deep,
Causing tremendous pressure,
And the very stones to weep.

So the feelings inside
Are building up so strong,
They are ripping the walls
That protected me all along.

When the pressure builds
Beyond its capacity to contain,
The volcano violently erupts
Spewing its contents like rain.

The pressure inside me
Is building to this place,
Where very soon one day my fear
Will glare into my face.

The fear of an eruption
Coming from so deep,
Must be faced directly;
No more pretense I can keep.

Even a sleeping mountain
Can slumber just so long,
And then the pressure builds,
To roar a brand new song.

Facing this scary reality
Is more than I can take.
But I must let go and erupt,
Or my life will be a fake.

So this waking volcano
That is inside of me,
Is about to erupt
And I fear what I will see.

And worst of all is
I can't force it to blow.
I know what needs doing,
But the doing is so slow.

Not only is it slow,
But very painful and intense.
The pressure has to build
Like a murder novel suspense.

At what place is it,
Where the breaking point in me
Allows my pent up feelings
To erupt to set me free?

It seems that with me
Before I'm able to explode,
I have to be pushed beyond
The point where I'll implode.

I don't really know
What God has got in store,
But I do know for sure:
His love will see me through more.

BARRIERS TO HEALING

Denial

I cannot see the path clearly
That lies ahead of me;
For my eyes are so blind
From denial that is filling me.

So I pretend to walk
This path ahead of me;
But I constantly stumble
Over obstacles I refuse to see.

I fall in a hole
But pretend it does not exist.
I hit a big rock;
Even in pain I persist.

How can I admit
I have blindly stumbled along?
To know that I have fallen
And that I am not strong?

But therein lies the secret:
To choose to clearly see
Every obstacle in my path,
For then can I walk free.

As long as I walk blindly
Pretending everything is fine,
Shame and pride will always
Overflow in this heart of mine.

THE PULL OF DEPRESSION

The Abyss

I have often seen
A dark abyss so deep,
Paralyzing me with fear,
I couldn't even weep.

Now I see it again,
Beckoning me to come.
Its darkness surrounds me,
I want to feel numb.

My fear turns to terror,
But I can't struggle alone . . .
It's much too powerful,
My mind can only moan.

The abyss' suffocating hold
Is strong and so real.
It wants me dead,
And gives me no time to heal.

I'm totally alone
With this monster inside.
There's no more place
For me to go hide.

Its darkness has wrapped
Itself around me;
And all I feel
Is cloaking darkness I cannot see.

The darkness pulls me deeper
How do I fight?
My strength is waning,
The darkness holds me tight.

I scream so loudly,
But no one hears.
Totally abandoned
In darkness and fear.

Mommy, why don't you
Hold me near?
I am so scared
And so alone in my fear!

I hurt so much
Deep inside of me.
I keep on crying.
Why can't you see?

I need you mommy!
Do you hear?
I am so alone,
I feel my lonely tears.

I can't stop crying
And feeling sad.
I don't like it at all,
Feeling so bad.

Why aren't you here?
I suck my thumb
And curl up tight.
Why won't you come?

Don't you see
My pain and fear?
I call you, and call you,
But you don't hear.

*I hurt right in my heart,
I don't know why.
It's a real bad pain,
And I feel like I'll die.*

*Mommy, LOOK AT ME!!!
I cry and scream!
You turn away . . .
How can you be so mean?!*

*I hate you Mommy!
I feel so cold.
And alone, all alone,
Alone, alone, and so very cold . . .*

ANXIETY

DRC '95

My Battle With Control

Control is the way
I handled my life,
To become independent
Through all the strife.

But I became obsessed
With doing things well;
Perfection was all that mattered.
Anything less was hell.

For that is how I felt;
My body didn't work well.
So to keep my life together,
Around me I built a shell.

A shell world of fantasy
For my mind was fine;
I felt in complete control
In this pretend world of mine.

"There's nothing you can't do"
My parents encouraged me.
So throughout all my days,
Control became the key.

I had to keep it together
Throughout each and every day;
And as I began to get older,
Stress even overtook play.

I began to pray and ask God
To help me to let go.
I wanted God in control
So my life could gently flow.

Slowly, one by one,
I made the choices to be free
And let go of the areas
That had such a grip on me.

But it was a long battle
I couldn't fight alone, you see.
There were other forces
At work deep inside of me.

To let go of my control
I had to make the choice
To ask help from others,
To give my needs a voice.

This choice I made
Weakened my controlling grip,
And I began to feel freer,
Giving control the slip.

But...I still needed to be free
Of the dark forces inside me
That held my mind captive
All these years, I now clearly see.

Through the help of a friend,
God chose to set me free,
By smashing each dark force
And making each one flee.

Each of these dark forces
Had their own name:
Anxiety, pain and fear.
Each forced to flee in Jesus' name.

The key to all this was
My desire to break loose,
Take the first step, thus
Loosening the noose.

This was a difficult lesson
For me to have to learn.
Letting go of my control
Gave my life a fresh turn.

It took God's power
To do this work in me;
So I give Him all the glory
For He has set me free.

WITHDRAW — FLASHBACK (confusion) 30 Dec 95

Pit Of Depression

Sinking feeling . . .
Falling deep,
Into darkness,
I just weep.

Never ending . . .
Torment and shame,
Agony builds,
I'm not the same.

This darkened state . . .
So very bleak,
A way out
I desperately seek.

Feeling lost . . .
Surrounded by fear.
Where is God?
I cannot hear.

The firm ground . . .
Where did it go?
Continuous falling,
I feel so low.

Powerless . . .
To come out;
Can God help?
I must not doubt.

I am stuck . . .
In this abyss.
There is no way
Out of this.

Darkness chokes . . .
My every breath.
How will relief come?
Only through death?

No!! Rescue comes . . .
To deliver me!
Only God
Can set me free!

And He will . . .
In His time.
I must wait;
Healing will be mine!

HOPELESSNESS
DESPAIR
ANGUISH
DEPRESSION
CORINA
ZALACE
2001

Depression Deep

Deep abyss,
Yawning darkness,
Unclimbable pit,
Strangling harness.

Pulling me down,
Down, down, down,
Deeper and deeper,
Until I drown.

Energy sapped,
Paralytic storm,
Responses slowed,
Emotions swarm.

Silenced words,
Stifling confinement.
Withdrawing inward
Self-defilement.

Destruction, devastation,
Swirling turmoil,
Despairing horror,
I recoil.

Numbing agony,
Squeezing my heart
Despairing depression,
Dreams thwart.

Lifeless colors,
Grays and black,
Hope destroyed,
Inner being wracked

Owning My Feelings

Feelings building
Deep inside me.
Let them out? How?
How to be free?!

Own my feelings?
Each and every one?
What about anger?
That's an ugly one!

And what about sadness,
And guilt and shame
Own those too?
Is this some sick game?

Ignore them all . . .
How else can I survive?!
These feelings are awful
And mess up my life.

Pressure keeps building;
I'm feeling much worse.
Every little thing
Triggers me, and I curse.

You say I feel bad
Because I ignore my feelings?
That I must recognize each one
In order to receive healings?

So, they're a part of me
And will never leave me?
Unless I recognize them
I can't become free?

I must claim them,
Not deny any at all.
If I continue to deny,
I'll never heal, but fall?

I guess I can't let go
Of something I deny.
Ignoring them won't work,
No matter how hard I try.

OK, I'll embrace loneliness
With its sadness and despair,
But with its hopelessness.
It's all too much to bear.

But as I embrace my feelings,
I now can see
My tears wash me clean
And bring healing to me.

I can now embrace my fear
With all its anxiety,
Magnified horrors
Make my courage atrophy.

But my fear turned around
Gives me wisdom
And shows me clearly where
Good and bad came from.

And now for anger
With its awful rage,
And resentment deep inside,
That traps me in a cage.

But as I embrace anger,
I feel a strong power
That gives me the strength
To change and not cower.

Guilt is the next feeling;
It held me captive so long,
Always making me do and be
What others wanted to prolong.

Now that I embrace guilt
A different side I see.
I am who I am, not perfect
But strong enough to just be me.

The last feeling is shame
With all its self-hate,
And low self-esteem.
I thought it would my life negate.

But now embracing shame,
Has made my life free
Making me approachable, so
My true self others can see.

Owning my feelings
Will surely guarantee
That all of my feelings
Can no longer own me.

My feelings will help me
To become who I am.
Liking me as me
Not a shadow wrapped in a sham.

My Many Faces

So many faces
That I wear
To hide behind.
But do I dare?

Dare to peel
Away the lie
That hides the question
"Who am I?"

So many secrets
Hidden very deep.
Shamed by them,
I just weep.

Fears abound
Deep down inside,
Holding me captive,
Smashing my pride.

So many barriers
Rise up to protect
The secrets and fears,
My shame did erect.

Removing the barrier
Of denial so strong,
Exposes the secrets
That stifled my song.

Only by exposing
My secrets and tears,
Can examination cleanse,
And heal my many fears.

For deep inside
I will find me;
The real me, hidden,
That none of us can see.

Why would I hide
Who I am,
Holding back all feelings
Like water trapped behind a dam?

Pain so intense
Deep and burning,
Covering up
All my feelings churning.

So, my many faces
Hide the real me away,
But I am learning
All these masks to weigh.

To just be me,
And to not pretend,
But face my pain
That never seems to end.

My many faces
Will still be there,
But now transparent,
Like the air.

SHAME

Dec '95

False Masks

I wear many masks
Each and every day,
Changing them often
For each person I portray.

The mask called strength
Is my favorite one.
Behind it I face any pressure
And cannot be undone.

Another favorite mask
Is my happy face.
It is always smiling . . .
No matter what I face.

Then there is the mask
Of piety masking pride;
Reflecting "holy" expressions,
Showing my "perfect" side.

My mask called brave
Makes me look very good.
Admired by many, but behind it
I'm hidden 'neath falsehood.

How others see me
Is a very great big deal,
But sad, as behind my masks
I am not able to be real.

My family all plays roles,
We have no choice, you see.
Each has their scripts and masks;
Our task to act the perfect family.

So much energy spent
Holding up each fancy mask,
Consuming all my hours,
Molded by this fruitless heavy task.

I know no other way
To face people, to face each day;
But gradually my masks
Crack like dried river clay.

Frantically I patch
The cracks that I can see;
Desperate to keep hiding
Behind masks that define "me".

But the cracks grow daily
And soon my brave mask breaks.
Another follows quickly;
My whole self-image aches.

As each mask crumbles,
I cry out in fear.
Now everyone will see
The real me very clear.

Then in sorrow I discover
What I've hidden all along;
First shame, then guilt helped make,
My insecurity so strong.

Within my insecurity,
I see what I have protected.
Unhealed hurts, unmet needs . . .
By all was I affected.

I did not seek out my masks.
They were thrust upon me
By a "loving" family that
Said all must "normal" be.

With all my needs and hurts,
So much pain I feel.
But I risk laying masks aside,
So God can finally heal.

So one by one I throw
Each broken mask before my feet.
I cast them down, choosing to live
A life free of self-defeat.

Now all my broken family masks
Are staring up at me,
The broken pieces, now stripped of deceit:
No longer have a hold on me.

And now I am truly free,
No more false masks defining me!
I can enjoy every day;
At last I can be me!!!!

ANGER

Anger

Anger
Blinding rage
Trapped
As in a cage

Trapped
In this fury
No escape
I worry

Spewing,
Hot words
Expressing
Deep hurts

Hiding
My face
Feeling
Disgrace

Ugly
I feel
Anger
So real

Release
Must find
Denial
Makes blind

Blind
To reality
Hiding
Behind rationality

Breaking
Defenses
My body
Tenses

Reality
So stark
Light
Penetrates dark

Truth
So freeing
Clearer
I'm seeing

Anger
Validated
Fury
Dissipated

Calmness
Inside
Peace
Resides

HIDING & WITHDRAWING (SHAME) 2 Jan. '96

My Wall Of Shame

Over many years
I have built a wall,
That surrounds my heart,
Very high and tall.

My wall protects me
From all pain and fear
Inflicted on me
By any who come near.

It is a powerful wall,
Around my stronghold,
Full of defenses, denial,
And secrets untold.

It fences in my many
Justifications, guilt
And unresolved angers
That over the years built.

It also circles round
My many unmet needs,
And unhealed hurts
That sprouted up like weeds.

With time they grew tall
And 'twined through my life;
My self-criticism and control
Creating bondage and strife.

One day God showed me
My unsurrendered soul
That needed to be sacrificed
For me to be made whole.

He said that my wall
Is a wall of shame.
It keeps my hurts hidden
And my needs unclaimed.

It is so very easy to blame
Satan for my behavior,
But what I really need
Is a healing Savior.

So I lay my soul
At the foot of the cross,
And count all things
As nothing but loss.

My wall of shame
Begins to slowly crumble
As I accept myself,
Even though I often stumble.

God's healing grace
Flows deep through my pain.
His everlasting mercy
Lets not one need remain.

The Games We Play

We'll do anything to keep
From having to feel
The pain inside of us
And having to deal.

We have our masks,
Our roles we play;
Our fantasies and addictions
That help us hide each day.

Our dysfunctional behavior
Not only hurts us,
But also creates emotional cuts
In those around us.

The games we play daily
And the many ways we hide,
All, so we don't have to
Feel the pain deep inside.

So we keep on walking
Down this denial road;
The road that leads nowhere
And increases our load.

We rationalize our behavior
In our avoidance life;
And we intellectualize,
Hiding our inner strife.

Yet, all this behavior
Creates ever more pain and shame,
Depression, guilt, rejection,
Self-hatred and continual blame.

We would rather listen
With our head,
Rather than listen
To our heart instead.

What is your heart
Really saying to you?
Can you drop the facade
And become the real you?

A very hard decision, but
A choice that you can make.
I know, for I did it with God.
This decision you cannot fake.

And what a work
God did in me,
Exposing the real person
And setting me free.

My Life's Survival

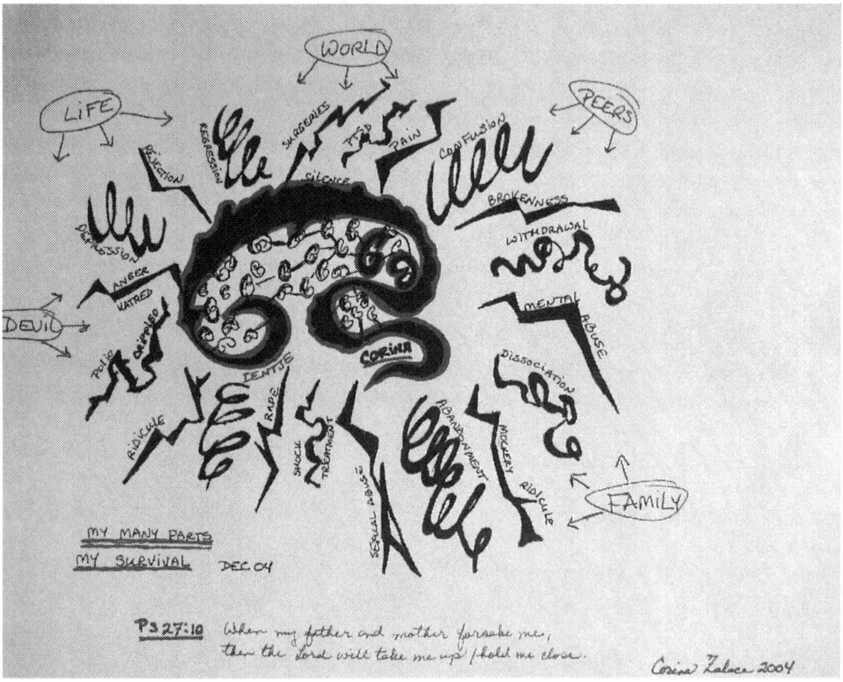
WORLD
LIFE
PEERS
DEVIL
FAMILY
REGRESSION
SURGERIES
PTSD
PAIN
CONFUSION
REJECTION
SILENCE
BROKENNESS
WITHDRAWAL
DEPRESSION
ANGER
HATRED
MENTAL ABUSE
CRIPPLED
POLIO
IDENTJE
CORINA
DISSOCIATION
RAPE
RIDICULE
SHOCK TREATMENT
ABANDONMENT
MOCKERY
RIDICULE
SEXUAL ABUSE
MY MANY PARTS
MY SURVIVAL
DEC 04
PS 27:10
When my father and mother forsake me,
then the Lord will take me up / hold me close.
Corina Zalaca 2004

Part One: Preface

Some of the things
That happened to me
Were so traumatic
They tinged my world darkly.

A handicap since age two
That started all my shame,
Then life became a constant struggle,
And I took all the blame.

With ninety plus surgeries behind me,
Pain became my way of life,
And reacting with unhealthy behavior
Filled my days with strife.

Molested at age five,
Three rapes when I was seven,
Made daily life often a horror,
I sought refuge in a fantasy haven.

A severe eating disorder,
Painkillers to numb out,
All this almost killed me
And left my life in doubt.

So many of my poems
Recount my awful walk,
Of coming out of darkness
And the misery of which I talk.

Part Two: The River

I saw myself in a river
Crystal clear and pure,
As the waters gently flowed;
Their embrace made me feel secure.

But then God took a stick
And stirred the bottom sand;
And all that clear water
Became murky by His hand.

That pure clear water
Became murky swirls,
Engulfing me completely
In its cloudy, darkening whorls.

It pulled me mercilessly
Into a hidden world of shame,
Overwhelming me with darkness;
My hopes all turned to blame.

But slowly over time,
God sifted through the muck,
And has been removing it
Until I become clean and unstuck.

Some debris is still left;
God isn't finished yet.
But the water is clearer
And daily will more pure get.

my body – Broken
from my handicap
+ my frustrations

27 August 1996

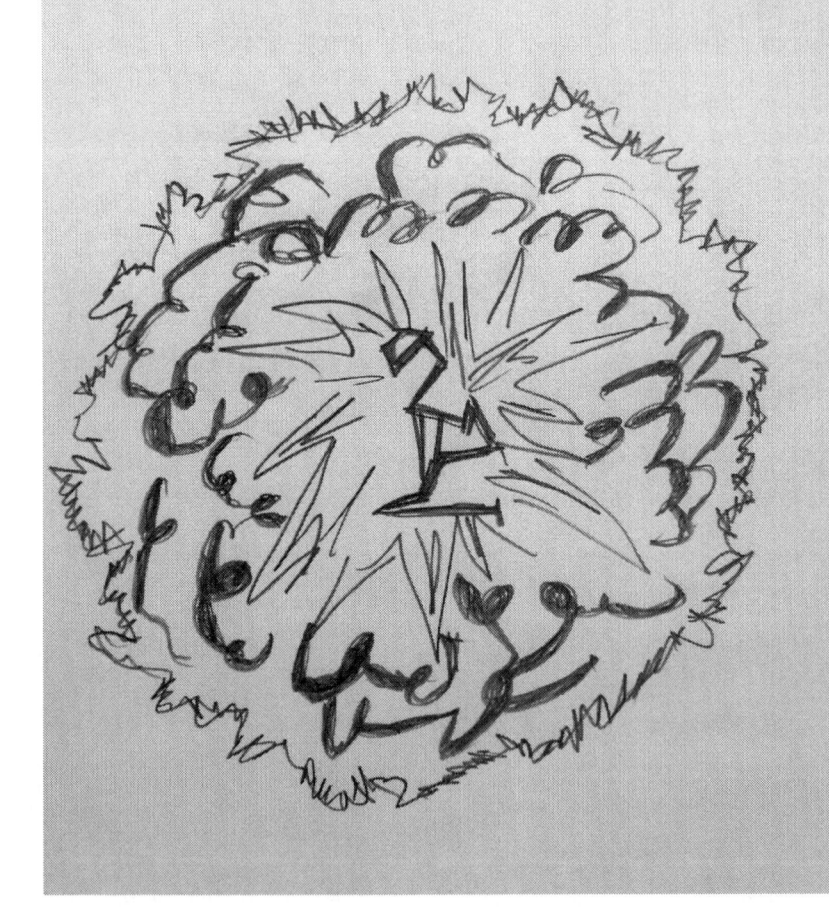

Part Three: My Handicap

I grew up feeling
Odd and out of place,
Not fitting in
Or deserving God's grace.

Stares of many people
I came to despise;
Ridicule and taunting
Crushed me like a vise.

Feeling mocking eyes upon me,
Like some Carney on display,
My bad leg kept me limping
Every step of every day.

The pain of rejection
Was far too much to bear.
I just could not handle
That no one seemed to care.

So I built a wall.
High and strong around me;
And I hid behind it,
And inside no one could see.

No one could see my incredible pain
And bottomless pit of shame
From my shabby treatment,
And I mistakenly took all the blame.

Blame for my handicap,
Not accepting who I am.
Because of all the ridicule,
My fortress wall became a dam.

All my harsh feelings locked up,
Including unrelenting pain.
For I did not feel safe to look upon them
Still blinded by an unjust stain.

Then God opened my eyes
To see that my wall
Was a wall of shame
That only kept me in thrall.

It kept me from receiving
The love and healing
I so badly needed
To resolve all my feelings.

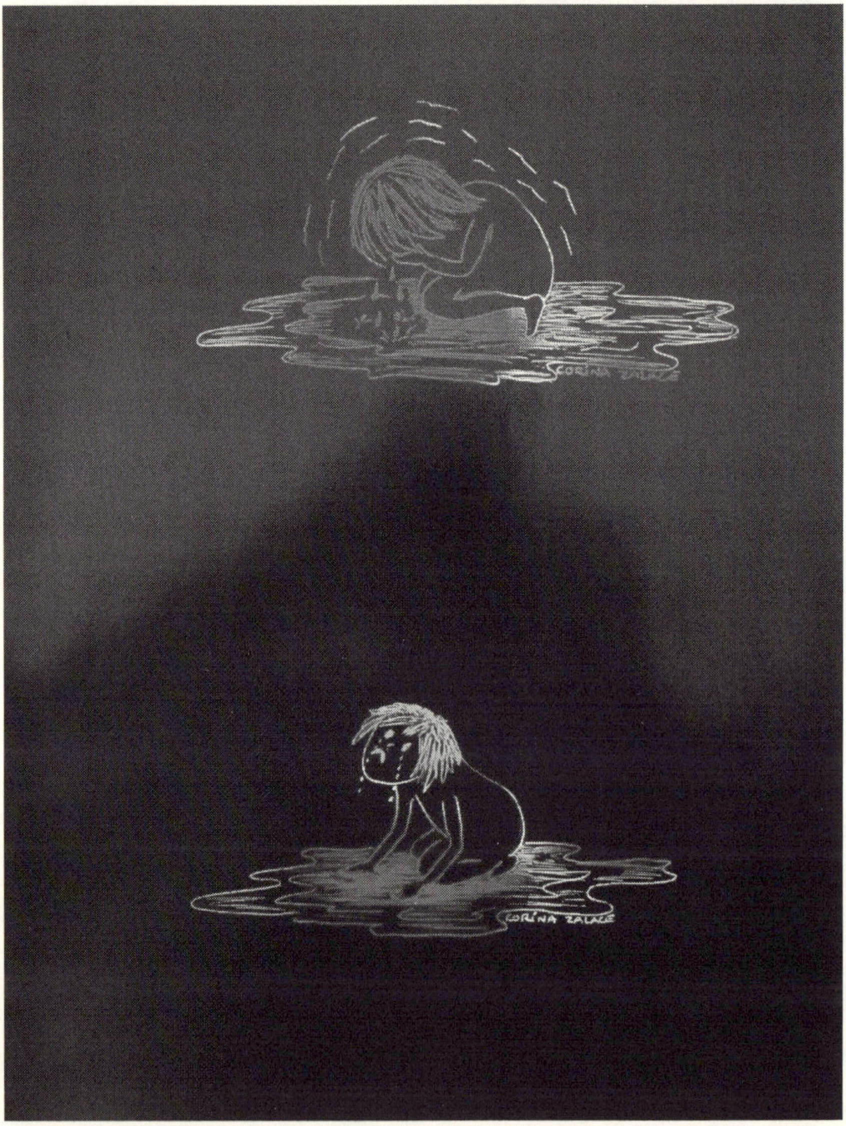
CORINA ZALACE
CORINA ZALACE

Part Four:
My Hiding Place

Deep in a dark cave
I hide out all alone.
So much pain and fear of others
Now leaves me by myself facing the unknown.

I tell myself I am quite content
To hide here all my life.
In this cave no one can hurt me,
Yet, my mind is roiled by strife.

One day I have a Visitor
Who comes and sits by me.
He tells me it is time
To set aside fear and be free.

Terror fills my being.
If I come out of my hideout,
Where will I hide when
Threatened and need a redoubt?

He assures me that He
Will never leave my side;
And then gives me His arm
And says the world we can bestride.

Slowly we begin to walk
Forth out of my hiding place.
To His arm I cling
And in His side bury my face.

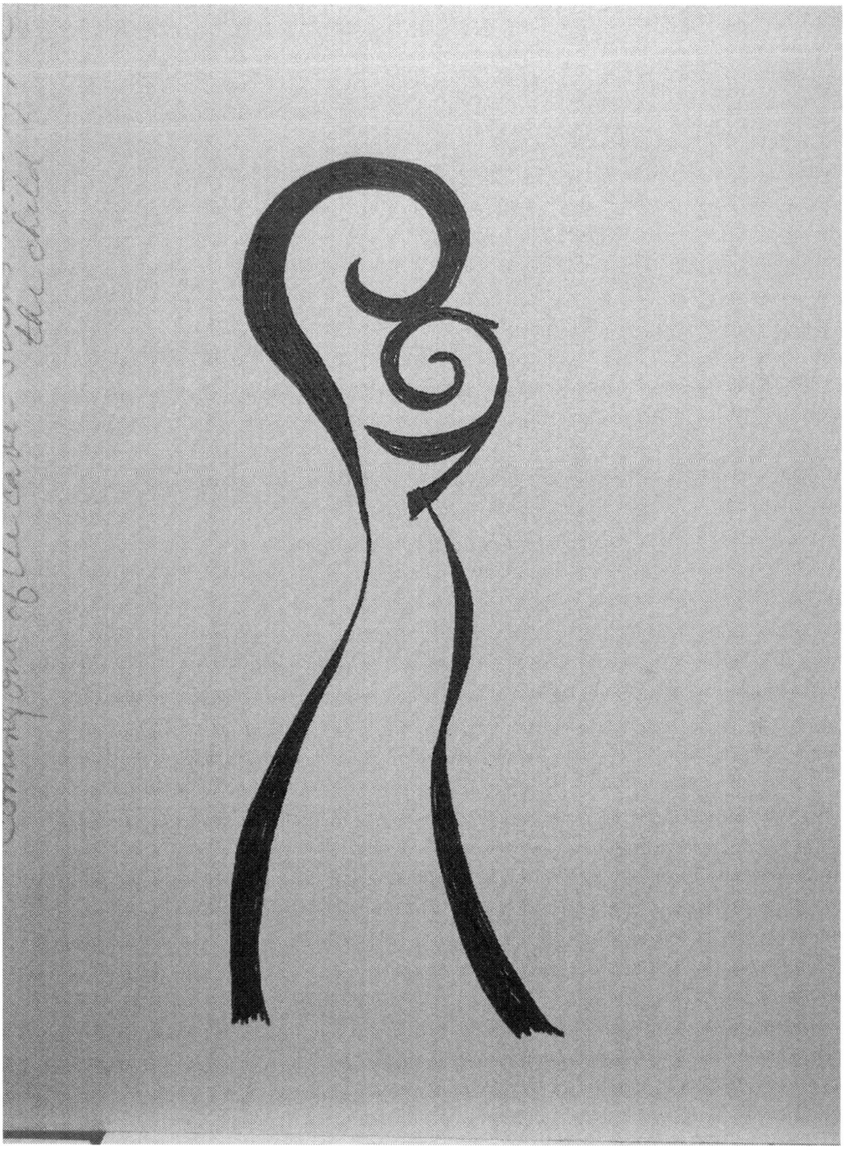

It takes a very long while
To come forth from my cave so deep.
And when we finally reach the light,
All I can do is weep.

Where will I go now
When I hurt or feel fear?
My Visitor gently lifts my face
And wipes away a tear.

I see my Heavenly Father;
And He is so full of love.
He says "Just press into Me...
I am your hiding place from above".

All of us hide at times...
What place do you hide within?
Follow your Heavenly Father
So you can your new life begin.

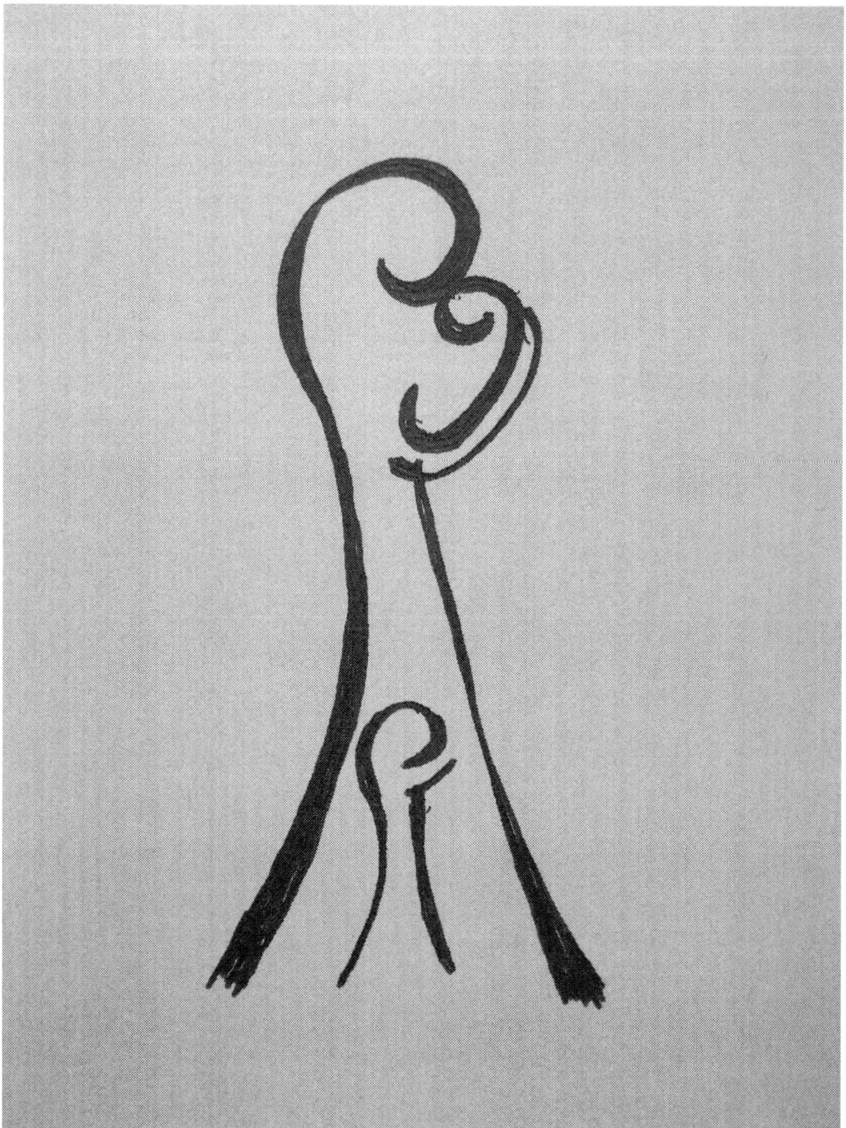

Part Five: The Secret

❧

Miserably the inner child sits,
Huddled and alone;
Trembling and shaking,
Every breath a tortured groan.

So much pain she suffered
Through all her years,
Pain that has kept her
Imprisoned by her fears.

The wall composed of parts,
Thinks it is protecting her,
For many of her memories
Are gone or at most a blur.

But then the many voices
In this "protective" wall,
Begin to speak out loud,
Sowing confusion as they call.

Revolting feelings are voiced
By these many mouths so loud.
What is behind this wall?
Why is this shame allowed?

The mouths all continue
To clamor on non-stop;
But there is one mouth
That lets a single secret drop.

She keeps this inner child silent
And curls her up in a ball,
So all will go away
And she will remain so small.

But what she is desperately hiding
Is a memory buried very deep,
It has been banished
For the pain makes her weep.

So much shame heaped upon her,
She dares not even look
At what lurks behind the wall--
For her innocence he took.

It takes the hand of Jesus
To show her behind this wall
And point her to the memory . . .
So to Jesus she calls.

What she sees revolts her
And she clings to Him.
She must see it all
To be healed deep within.

Recovering from surgery,
She is only five years old.
When he molested her,
So selfish, so uncaring, so cold.

Again at age seven
Three times she was raped.
Heartless deeds, devastating forces
Driving how she was reshaped.

To survive what was happening
She flees the scene searing through her mind
And goes to a pleasant place
Leaving all the horror behind.

For more than three and fifty years,
Until a time as this,
The memories remained hidden;
As if nothing were amiss.

But Jesus knew that sins like this
Had to face the light.
They could no longer hide
From the brightness of Son light.

So Jesus lifts her up
And gently strokes her hair;
Although this all happened,
His healing hands say "I care".

Even though I am His child,
I must face worldly harm and pain;
But through all of it
His healing and love will sustain.

So the shame and pain of memories
Fade completely in His love,
The inner child forgives her abusers
As healing settles on her like a dove.

Part Six: The Silence

For most of my life
My inner child was locked
Deep inside of me . . .
All emotions were blocked.

I felt nothing at all,
Hiding all behind smiles.
It was my family's way
To face each of life's trials.

Yet, the little voice inside
Was screaming loud and clear;
But no sound came out,
To show my anxiety and fear.

So many different masks
I had to wear to hide
What really was happening
Deep down inside?

Oh, how my little child
Wanted to be heard,
But no one was safe for her,
So silently she floundered.

Her pain did come out
In very destructive ways,
With self-abuse and bulemia
Causing agonizing pain most days.

Anything to "see" the pain
On my body somewhere;
Then I knew I was alive
And did feel something there.

My image of myself
Was so incredibly low,
I just wanted to fade away.
I hated myself so.

And so from early on
I created a secret cave
Deep inside of me where
I could pretend that I was brave.

Hiding there so often,
I felt strong and brave.
No one could touch me
Or hurt me in my cave.

It took the hand of Jesus,
To walk me out of my cave,
For it had become my prison,
Keeping me bound, not brave.

Part Seven: Who Am I?

When I was hurt beyond words
As a child growing up,
My mind split off parts
To protect itself from breakup.

A large wall composed
Of my many parts,
Bound together strong
Like veins of gold in quartz.

Some parts are good,
Some are bad;
And together they make,
The happy and the sad.

Each split-off part
Is still a part of me;
And yet each is a brick in a wall
Over which one cannot see.

All these bricks have voices,
And each their own name,
With their own identity
And place in my wall of shame.

There is a major brick
The leader of them all.
This leader's name is lentje
The cornerstone of my wall.

This wall of many bricks
With names like shame,
Loser, worthless and rejection,
Humiliated, betrayed and blame.

The more and more I strove
To be heard and seen,
The more I got put down by
Friends and family acting mean.

Each painful incident
Stabbed my already bleeding heart;
My wall of shame grew higher
And stronger with each dart.

Deeper I retreated
Behind my wall of shame,
All the while thinking
It was I who was to blame.

Two powerful bricks
Who helped lentje escape,
Were Silence and Dissociate.
Breakout artists both, no jape.

Silence was given the power
To hide each and every other part,
Burying who I really am,
Ever deeper within my heart.

Each brick began to hide
Behind its self-made mask;
Hiding their true identity
Became the safest task.

But Silence had a partner;
Dissociate was her name.
Her job was to help
Me play a pain-deadening game.

Whenever I got hurt badly,
Dissociate whisked me away
To a corner of my imagination
Far, far above the fray.

She also met all my needs
By giving me a different life
Of fantasy and make-believe,
Free from any strife.

In this new "real life",
I felt no more pain,
And every need was met.
A happy life I would feign.

So Silence and Dissociate
Worked great as a pair.
With lentje's consent,
They did more than their share.

Honesty was not an option,
It was unacceptable you see;
For honesty would completely
And totally expose and destroy me.

Every brick was my friend
And did all to protect me;
They helped me to survive,
Even in a sick way, as I now see.

But one day the time arrived
When my brick's masks
Began to crack and crumble,
Laying waste all their tasks.

After all the masks lay
In pieces before each brick;
Each stared back at me a mask of deceit.
These masks had made my life toxic.

Silence was suddenly exposed,
For gone was her mask.
Masks were no longer needed
For my hidden truths were unmasked.

Silence was hurting badly,
Feeling abandoned and alone.
She felt like a nobody,
"I'm worthless!" she would moan.

Then Jesus came to Silence
And asked her for her trust;
But she is afraid to give it,
For He might drop it in the dust.

Jesus comforts Silence
His words like a rampart.
He wants her to trust Him:
His words her hope's counterpart.

So Silence gives Him
Her slowly bleeding heart.
And He carefully places it
Beside his own pure heart.

WOW! She and Jesus' hearts
Beat together as one.
He will never fail her;
She can finally see the Son.

Silence decides to ask Jesus
For a brand new name.
"Confidence" He names her.
And she has never been the same.

Confidence then notices
Dissociate her friend;
She sees her hurting heart
And knows she needs a godsend.

Dissociate becomes defensive;
She has done all she could.
Helping me to pretend by
Prompting me since childhood.

But then she realizes
Without Silence there,
She has no need to pretend,
So she lays her heart bare.

Confidence holds her hand
As Dissociate waits for her name.
Jesus calls her "Reality".
And she is finally freed from shame.

The shame kept her hidden
Deep within a fantasy life;
But now with Confidence,
She feels no more strife.

All the other bricks,
The good and bad alike,
Now all seem to come together
Making the stronger self I like.

Each brick works together
Making me who I am,
Able to face anything
And resist every scam.

Our hearts beating as one
In Jesus we all now hide,
For when troubles come,
In Him we now truly abide.

As I continue to heal,
My brick wall of shame, it seems,
Is becoming a huge wall
Of diamonds that all gleam.

With each passing day,
A healthier stronger person I become;
Knowing who I am
In Christ I am no longer numb!

Hurt

Silence   Shame

Part Eight:
My Left Over Pain

Now that I don't need
Silence and escape any more,
I am surprised to find
What lies deep in my heart's core.

Pain so unimaginable,
So searing and so deep,
My heart feels split in half;
All I can do is weep.

Heaving gut-wrenching sobs,
Like a dam bursting wide;
The tears flow non-stop,
My pain I can no longer hide.

The lifetime of pain
That filled my heart;
Now has to come out;
And is tearing me apart.

I feel like I'm dying,
The pain is so intense.
I can hardly breathe,
Anticipating the consequence.

I reach out to a friend,
Who is there for me.
Together we call on Jesus
To help set me free.

All of a sudden I see Him,
Holding His arms open wide.
He says "Come here My child".
In Him I am sanctified.

He lifts me in His arms
And holds me very close.
His peace and comfort
Calm my fears and woes.

He calls my friend over
For a group hug.
I feel so protected,
Their love holds me snug.

Jesus then tells me:

"Lest it overwhelm you,
The pain must come out
Slowly in My time;
Do not burden yourself with doubt."

I will not leave you
And neither will your friend,
As you allow your tears to flow,
Slowly your heart I will mend".

"Your heart is still torn
By your intense lifetime pain,
But as I gather each tear,
It will be healed without stain."

As I hear His words,
I continue to weep;
With each searing hot tear,
I can feel the pain so deep.

Yet, as each tear flows,
Some of my pain leaves,
Even though my crying
Comes in sobbing heaves.

I have accepted that
Grieving takes a long time;
As I rest in God's hands,
I will be healed for a lifetime.

It has been quite a journey,
Painful and headlong;
But with each agonizing step,
God is making me free and strong.

Halleluiah!!
Praise be to Him alone!!!

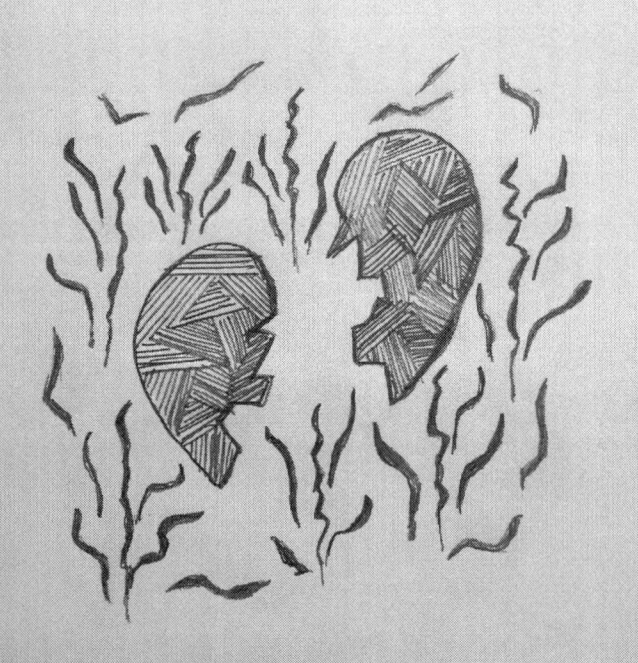

TORN HEART

Dec '95

My Heart's Cry

What is life worth, God,
Without Your presence?
Am I being tested
With so many lessons?

God, I am willing
Even right now.
When times are bad
You'll make good somehow.

Don't give up on me,
I cry and plead.
For deep down inside
It is You I really need.

I think what You
Would like to hear
Is how much I love You
And how I want You near.

Oh Jesus, I love You;
I give You my all.
I'm a broken vessel,
Scattered shards after my fall.

Mine was a hard fall,
Filled with agony and pain;
But all I need to see, Lord
Is when You were slain.

Slain just for me,
Which I cannot comprehend.
Such an intense love,
Understanding cannot transcend.

So I'll just receive
This love You have for me.
And Lord, I love You so
Because your love set me free.

Lord, I am listening
To hear what You say.
I need to be encouraged
By You in every way.

God is speaking
Ever so softly to me.
"You are who You are,
And I want you to be free.

"You are My treasure,
My chosen one.
I love you so deeply
And with Me you have won."

His voice continues,
Reassuring and calm.
His soothing words
Are like a healing balm.

"You are so precious,
The apple of My eye;
Made in My image,
You shall never die.

"You have chosen
To hide in Me.
I'll protect you
And set you free.

"I see you hurting,
Your life filled with dismay.
I see your struggles
Each and every day.

"In your darkness,
I am there.
In your confusion,
I will help you when you err.

"You can trust Me
Through your deep pain,
I'll never disappoint you.
My love will never wane."

GRIEF

Dec '95

Pain And Purpose

What do you do
When pain tears at you,
And it won't go away
No matter what you do?

When tears roll
Nonstop down your cheeks,
And relief won't come;
Because your pain just shrieks?

The only answer then
Is to look to the cross.
Jesus died on it;
His life was not a loss.

His broken body
Became the bread,
So that many could come
To Him to be fed.

His spilt blood
At such high cost,
Sets men free
And rescues the lost.

So when you hurt,
Broken and frail you feel,
Look to the cross
Where His blood and pain heal.

*Broken bread
And poured out wine,
Becomes your life
By God's design.*

My Purpose In Life

When nothing in my life
Made sense anymore,
And all I thought worthwhile
I could no longer but deplore . . .

When the meaning of life
Was taken from me,
And everything I did
Had no purpose I could see . . .

When all my ambitions
Had run seriously aground,
And all my goals
I realized were unsound . . .

When all my desire
Was blotted out,
And I did not know
What my life was about . . .

When despair engulfed
My whole being,
And darkness so thick
Was all that I was seeing . . .

When all I felt
Was hopelessness inside,
And nothing but aimlessness
In me did abide . . .

When all I deserve
Was absolutely nothing at all,
And because of my failures
Into a hole I should crawl . . .

When guilt and shame
Filled every part of me,
I struggled to please
Everyone I did see . . .

When anger so intense
Was boiling inside,
And was impossible to release
But I found I could not hide . . .

When failure overwhelmed
Every effort of mine,
And between helplessness and
Hopelessness I sought a lifeline . . .

When this deep pit
Had swallowed me,
And its slimy steep walls
Kept me from being free . . .

When I cried out
With all that I had,
And acknowledged defeat
I needed a Galahad . . .

When everything was dark
And the path I could not see,
My sense of purpose
In my life had escaped me . . .

Then did I remember
My prayer of years ago,
To fill a great desire
Is why I have suffered so . . .

I desired to be like Jesus
Who died on the cross for me
And shed His precious blood
For all mankind to see.

I was ever so willing
To suffer for His sake
And to know Him in His suffering
If that is what it would take.

To be broken bread
And poured out wine,
Had been my prayer
For which my heart did pine

Philippians 3:10

Old Messages-- New Messages

*"You are so ugly
When you are mad !
And I don't care
If you feel sad !"*

I am NOT ugly
When I am mad!!!
My feelings DO NOT
Make me bad!!!

*"Don't frown!
Put on a smile!
People are watching
So don't be vile!"*

I am in pain
Deep in my heart!
I can't smile now;
Your false world I will thwart!!

*"Perfection rules!
Don't do wrong,
By showing a face
That is so long!"*

*I don't care
What my face will show!!!
So many emotions
From my heart flow!!*

*As they flow,
I can't stop them!
So don't you
Dare to pre-condemn!!!*

**"You don't want others
To talk about you.
So you must smile
No matter what you do."**

*I don't want to
Focus on my fears,
And have to seek approval
From my peers!*

*I must listen
To what I need!
It is NOT selfish
If I want to succeed!!*

**"Things didn't happen
The way you say.
You have it wrong said Mom
When you speak this way."**

*But I remember things
In a child's simple way,
And what comes back to me
Is exactly what I'll say!*

"You should do this!
You must do that!
You have to be strong!
There's no time to have a spat!"

Don't pile all this
Right on top of me!
Because I'm not guilty,
For God has set me free!

I will no longer carry
All your guilt and blame!
I have my own pain,
So don't try to also pile on shame!

So many voices were
Shrieking in my head . . .
So many lies
I looked upon with dread.

But now there is sweet silence
And I can begin to think.
I now have healthy thoughts,
And with them I'm in sync!

B

From Down To Up!

My heart . . .
Is torn!
My past . . .
I mourn!

I grieve . . .
Lost dreams!
Lost strength and hopes . . .
Lost sunbeams!

A child . . .
So full of pain!
Helpless . . .
Tears fall like rain!

Abandoned . . .
So alone!
She suffers painfully . . .
And moans!

Endless . . .
Seems the pain!
Why . . .
Is the world inhumane?

Shame . . .
Desire to hide!
Handicapped . . .
Feeling awful inside!

Ugly . . .
Limping along!
Stared at . . .
Must stay strong!

Fear . . .
Leaving me scarred!
Like a vise . . .
Squeezing hard!

Death . . .
Stares at me!
So dark . . .
I can't see!

Pain . . .
Incredible pain!
Piercing . . .
Stabbing pain!

Depressed . . .
Sad!
No joy . . .
Feel so bad!

Volcanic . . .
Shaking mountaintop!
Pressure builds . . .
And doesn't stop!

God . . .
Where are You?
Deliver me . . .
My tormenters subdue!

A pit . . .
So deep!
Walls so high . . .
And so steep!

Stuck . . .
I can't breakout!
God, help me . . .
I shout!

Only God . . .
Reaches in!
Freedom granted . . .
In Him I win!

When . . .
Will I be free?
When . . .
Will I know me?

Agony . . .
Pure Hell!
Hollow . . .
Empty like a shell!

Goals . . .
Are lost!
No direction . . .
Storm-tossed!

Needs . . .
Not met!
Desperate . . .
To just forget!

Love . . .
Pure and true!
Come Fill me . . .
With life anew!

God . . .
Is love!
He comes . . .
Shining from above!

Only God . . .
Can fill me!
With acceptance . . .
Set me free!

Affirmations . . .
I must give!
To myself . . .
So I can live!

A letter . . .
Written!
My inner child . . .
Hidden!

Come out . . .
Be free!
I choose . . .
To be me!

Me . . .
The child!
Beautiful . . .
Not reviled!

To be . . .
Is OK!
I Enjoy . . .
Being me each day!

Special . . .
God's creation
Am I . . .
Celebration!

Joy . . .
Fills my life!
Vanquishes . . .
Pain and strife!

Grace

My conscience seared
By my sin,
Once again I stand
Before God, filled with chagrin

All my shame
Covers me;
And my guilt
Condemns me.

Pitching forward
On my face,
Bitter tears fall
For judgment I now face.

I wait for anger
From above,
But all I feel
Is His love.

As I look up
Into His face,
I see and I feel
Only mercy and grace.

Like a wave
Washing over me,
Cleansing my sin
And setting me free.

DEPRESSION
CREEPING
IN
&
OVERWHELMING   Dec '95

Hospital Nights

Darkness creeps in
As night falls.
Echoes bounce up and down
Dimly lit empty halls.

The squeaking of cartwheels,
Nurses dispensing meds,
Quieting the screaming pain
Exploding from all the beds.

Beeps of machines
Monitoring vital signs.
Poles and supports
Holding IV lines

Loneliness abounds here
Filling hours so long.
Feelings of abandonment
Overwhelm even the strong.

Unrelenting pain
Never stops its torment;
Cutting like a knife,
Resistance is spent.

Drug induced sleep
Brings welcome reprieve.
Soon nausea in waves
Begins to swell and heave.

Tears come easily.
Defenses are spent.
Fears are great
As emotions torment.

Someone's hand brushes mine
With a tender touch,
Exactly what's needed.
That's not asking too much.

A word of comfort,
Spoken from the heart,
Can soothe the pain
That rips my days apart.

Compassion is a gift
That anyone can give.
That little bit of special love
And helps the patient live.

My Gift

God spoke to me one day:

I have given you a quality,
A present unlike any other gift.
It is the gift of endurance,
And perseverance that give others a lift.

So often you suffer terribly,
Your pain seems more than you can bear;
But even if you don't feel me near,
I've wrapped you in my tender loving care.

Your pain is NEVER in vain,
Though it feels like being torn apart,
In the midst of your agony and torment,
Your tears are gems I treasure in my heart.

I feel each pain you suffer,
I hear your pleas for relief.
But the greatest gift you give Me
Is that you love me through your grief.

No matter how long the journey;
No matter how difficult the road;
Keep your eyes on Me always
And I will lighten your oppressive load.

I will not always straighten
The painful path you must follow.
But one thing I have always promised
Is that you will never walk it solo.

I love you, My child
More than you'll ever know,
So look to me and follow
Without fear or sorrow.

Letting Go

There is a storm
Raging in my heart,
Causing great unrest,
Tearing me apart.

My mind is racing,
My soul is in strife.
I cannot figure out
All this torment in my life.

I beat on the wall
That protects this pain,
But all my effort
To breach it is in vain.

Why won't this wall
Come crashing down for me?
I am at a loss;
Frustration overcomes me.

As I ponder how
To tear this wall apart,
A still small voice
Whispers in my heart.

"My Child, be still,
Let your spirit hear Me.
Your struggle is noisy,
And cannot set you free.

"Calm your soul
And sit before Me.
I will do the work
As you wait on Me.

"This place of waiting
Is consecrated by Me,
As you learn to watch
How I set you free.

"Confusion and busyness
Clutter your mind …
Your human wisdom
Only makes you blind.

"So sit and rest awhile,
And let Me show you
My way to victory
In everything you do.

"Let Me live My purpose
Completely through you.
Just rest in Me;
I will show you what to do."

PAIN & FEAR

Dec '95

My Pain

I hear . . .
Don't be depressed.
It could be worse;
Don't feel so stressed.

I hear . . .
You should feel blessed.
Your family and talents,
In Jesus you should rest.

Don't you see . . .
My pain, my life,
I must be allowed
To wrestle with this strife.

I shut you out . . .
When you try to fix me.
Your good intentions
Don't bring me peace, you see.

Do not deny . . .
My hurt, my pain.
Allow me to feel
So I can heal again.

Just hold . . .
My hand and by me stay.
Don't promise to come
And comfort me another day.

Your pain . . .
On seeing my pain,
Must be faced and felt, too,
Your comfort you can't feign.

Be there now for us . . .
So together we can heal,
Through this painful walk
As we face our pain so real.

If you won't . . .
Feel your pain, my pain,
I must pass you by so that
My effort won't have been in vain.

Abba Father

Abba Father,
Deep within I cry.
Hold me close,
I crave Your presence nearby.

I need Your touch,
Your very embrace;
When I look up
I need to see Your face.

Shame has kept me
From seeing what is true.
It made me hide
My face from You.

Yet, You kept loving
And accepting me.
And because of Jesus
You say that I am free.

For there is nothing
That I have done so fearsome
That I should hide
When You call "Come"

So I continue
To climb into Your lap,
And Your arms
Around me wrap.

*I never want You
To let go of me,
For only You know
What is best for me.*

B

My Vow

What is going on in me Lord?
I feel suffocated and bound,
As if I can hardly breathe
Or barely move around.

Then Jesus showed me
A vow I had made one day:
To protect myself always
From someone's abusive way.

I had said I would do
Whatever pleased him,
So he would not hurt me
If I should upset him.

I saw a thick metal chain
Wrapped around my neck;
The other end was in his hand,
To hold me in check.

I asked Jesus:

What do I do now?
How can I break free?
I don't want to be chained
From now until eternity.

Jesus reached out to me,
Taking my hand in His hand,
Touching the chain, it shattered,
As if it was but a flimsy strand.

Then Jesus touched the part
That around my neck was wrapped,
With but one finger gently,
And the chain immediately snapped.

The vow now was broken,
No longer chained to him was I,
Allowing God to work in me
Healing a life that had been a lie.

The lies that were thrust upon me
During my growing up years,
Would now be easily replaced
By God's truths, erasing all my fears.

But also it has set
Him free from me,
So God can work in him
And make him truly free.

Vows are very powerful
When said under duress.
They can keep us bound and chained
And fill our life with stress.

God takes vows very seriously,
With consequences we often can't see,
Until He opens our eyes
And in His name we can be set free.

Of course, there are vows we make
That are healthy and good; and
When God reveals an unhealthy one,
He guides us 'till we understand.

And that is what He did in me
To take away my unhealthy stress,
So I can live my life in peace
Bathed in God's daily largess.

₿

Will You Still Stand?

Will you still stand
When all you've known
Has been removed,
And you feel so all alone?

Will you still stand
When God's presence
Isn't there any more?
Can you live in His absence?

Will you still stand
When all that you were
Is devoured by God's fire as He
Teaches a lesson that to you is just a blur?

Will you still stand
When darkness engulfs you,
And it will not leave,
No matter what you do?

Will you still stand
When you can't stand tall,
And if God were not to hold you
Right on your face you'd fall?

Will you still stand
While you are sinking deep
Into a dark empty pit
And all you can do is weep?

Will you still stand
When your heart is broken,
And you can't feel or even hear
The words that God has spoken?

Will you still stand
When you feel so low,
Regardless of the blessings
On you God did bestow?

Will you still stand
When the joy of the Lord
Has been removed
And may never be restored?

Will you still stand
When Jesus calls,
As His fire burns defenses that
You've piled high like walls?

God asks: "Are you willing
To walk the extra mile with Me?
The road will be painful
But My love will set you free".

Can you say, like Job:
"Though He slay me,
Yet will I praise Him",
For only God's love will set me free.

HIDING IN JESUS
AS HE CARRIES ME

2007

God Is Still There

I stand in awe
Of Christ's work in me,
Changing me daily
And setting me free.

He was there for me
In a pit so deep,
When all I could do
Was weep and weep.

When all I could sense
Was darkness all around,
God was still there
Though my spirits were aground.

When I could not feel
His presence near,
He was still there
Though I was filled with fear.

No matter where I am
Or what I have to face,
God is still there
Showing me His grace.

It is easy to see God
When all is going well.
But, it is a walk of faith
When your life's a living hell.

God has shown me
He will always be there.
He will never fail me
His love says do not despair.

God's Incredible Joy

Joy . . . unspeakable joy
Bubbling up from within,
Moments of pure delight,
To be savored without chagrin.

My heart was dancing,
I felt such joy inside.
The most awesome feeling
Within my heart did abide.

What I felt wasn't happiness,
For my trials were great;
But God's supernatural joy
Within my heart would resonate.

Wait for His timing
And His perfect way.
With His joy in my heart,
I trusted Him through each day.

Then one day, suddenly
I got knocked down hard
By a "spiritual Mack Truck";
My whole outlook was jarred.

I cried out to God,
Not knowing what to do,
And waited for His insight
To help me make it through.

As He shared Job with me
And all that he went through,
God began to show me
Exactly what I must do.

I was to praise Him
Through my confusing trial.
So I obeyed Him gladly,
Praising Him all the while.

After several agonizing days
I began to feel myself again.
His joy returned in me and I knew
My prayers were answered, Amen!

I soon realized this attack
Was an extreme test,
And by obeying God
He sheltered me and I was blest.

His best gift to me is His joy
Bubbling up again with vim.
And His peace everlasting
Holding me secure in Him.

My Prayer--Psalm 63

God, O my God,
How earnestly I seek You.
You alone are my God.
My soul thirsts only for You.

Every part of me
Belongs to You alone.
With my praise and worship,
I give You me to own.

I've felt Your power
And gazed upon Your glory.
Your love is unfailing,
My testimony is Your story.

My hands lifted in prayer,
My life will honor You.
Only You can satisfy me;
I sing joyful songs of praise to You.

Sleepless nights I meditate on how
You've brought me through so many things.
And I sing for joy to You
In the shadow of Your wings.

I stay very close to You
Holding Your strong arm.
And now I feel secure because
You will keep me from all harm.

Psalm 91:1

How I long deeply
To dwell in God's shelter,
To get away from
Life's helter-skelter.

To live with Him
In quiet and peace,
So the frantic pace
Of my life will cease.

So I choose to move
Into God's space,
By giving Him my life
As I seek His face.

My heart quiets down,
I begin to feel content,
As I enjoy His presence,
Purely Heaven-sent.

Daily I learn from Him.
He becomes my best Friend,
As we live together
His presence a godsend.

But God asks of me
A deeper walk: to abide
In His constant presence
Where He can be my guide.

Yet, to abide there
I must give without chagrin
One more thing
From myself very deep within.

He asks of me to
Yield my total will,
Holding nothing back,
Letting go and being still.

For only by giving Him
My will and my all,
Can I move wherever
His shadow may fall.

He and I become one,
The Lord and me;
And it is amazing the
Spiritual truths I now see.

I feel more at peace
As He is my rest.
He bolsters my spirits
No matter how severe the test.

His presence calms me;
My spirit is still.
And this all because
I gave Him my will.

The Darkness

Do you feel aimless,
And hopeless beside?
Life seems so senseless
With all you try to hide?

No matter what you do,
God seems so far away,
Making all your pleading
Seem useless every day?

Many the times in my life
I feel robbed of any choice,
And darkness sweeps me away;
Stealing any hope I can rejoice.

Like being in a desert
With no end in sight;
I struggle to push on
With all of my might.

Yet the horizon is never
Within my grasp;
As I struggle forward,
I feel my last gasp.

Oh, how we hate
The dark times in our life.
We can't see a thing
In a world with terror rife.

Yet, there is so much
That happens in the dark
That can never occur
In daylight stark.

It is during the night
That we get our full rest,
Restoring our strength
To function at our best.

Also the stars shine brightest
In the darkness of night,
Letting us see the
Scintillation of their light.

Even during stormy days
Above those dark clouds swirling,
The sun shines brightly and
Streams across the skies till evening.

A film photographer develops
His photos in a darkroom,
Where pictures come to life,
Emerging from the gloom.

It is also in the dark,
Under soil so moist and rich,
That a seed can start life
Within its own protective niche.

God desires to draw us
To Himself during dark days,
To share His deep secrets
And show us His ways.

He wants us to know
And feel His deep love:
No matter how dark the pathway,
He protects us from above.

His voice is so gentle,
Comforting and wise.
He sees us as His treasure,
More cherished than any other prize.

But we are not meant
To blindly stumble along
Through life's dark valleys
Our troubles to prolong.

To reach the mountain top,
There are dark valleys to go through,
But even knowing that
Can't keep us from God's rendezvous.

So the next time you find
Yourself in a deep dark valley,
Remember that some things are not
Learned except by facing life bravely.

Choices

Do you ever wonder
Why at times we suffer so?
Why God allows pain
And burdens of woe?

His reasons so often
Are hard to understand.
We cry and we yell and
All the while misunderstand.

Yet He gives us a choice
With each situation we must face.
We can choose to become bitter
Or better, filled with grace.

There are many daily obstacles,
Yet our attitude speaks loud.
How will we handle it?
Will we be grateful or cowed?

We can be successful
By never giving up;
Or we can resist learning
Life's lessons and never shapeup.

We have examples in life
That can teach us a lot.
Especially in nature
Keen lessons has God taught.

A weed doesn't let its growth
Be stopped by a sidewalk
But slowly and unyieldingly
Splits asunder this man-made rock.

And a diamond is formed
By intense heat and pressures
Deep in the earth's bowels, becoming
One of the world's great treasures.

Waves crashing relentlessly
Against the shoreline rock,
Grind down their rough edges
And their very hardness mock.

And water dripping mercilessly
On the bottom of a sink
Eventually will wear it through
Plink by endless plink.

So as you can clearly see,
The choices are ours.
Each of life's struggles
Can make us superstars.

The power for us
Is to make a choice,
Whether positive or negative
Then we can have a voice.

Do we want to be bitter
Or better in this life.
Better if each daily challenge
Sees us addressing our strife.

When You Feel...

There is a secret
In the wisdom I give;
For if you obey Me,
Victorious you'll live!

SO...

When you feel down,
Praise Me!
When you feel confused...
Adore Me!

When you feel sad,
Worship Me!
When you feel scared,
Glory in Me!

When you feel hopeless,
Look to Me!
When you feel angry,
Shout out to Me!

When you feel depressed,
Cling to Me!
When you are hurting,
Sing to Me!

When you feel frustrated,
Thank Me!
When you feel lost,
Seek Me!

When you feel anxious,
Trust Me!
When you feel abandoned
Yearn for Me!

When you feel lonely,
Call for Me!
When you feel alone,
Hide in Me!

FOR...

When you praise Me,
You are worshipping Me!
When you cling to Me,
You are being held by Me

When you thank Me,
You are trusting Me !
When you call for Me,
You are hiding in Me!!

When you adore Me,
You glory in Me!
When you shout out to me?
It does not hurt Me!

When you seek Me,
You will find Me!

THEREFORE . . .

When you yearn for Me,
I am there for you.

When you suffer,
I will heal you!
With mercy and grace,
I will strengthen you!

Through your pain,
I will comfort you!
My perfect love,
Dispels all fear in you!

And joy of great value,
Will come to you!

Jesus

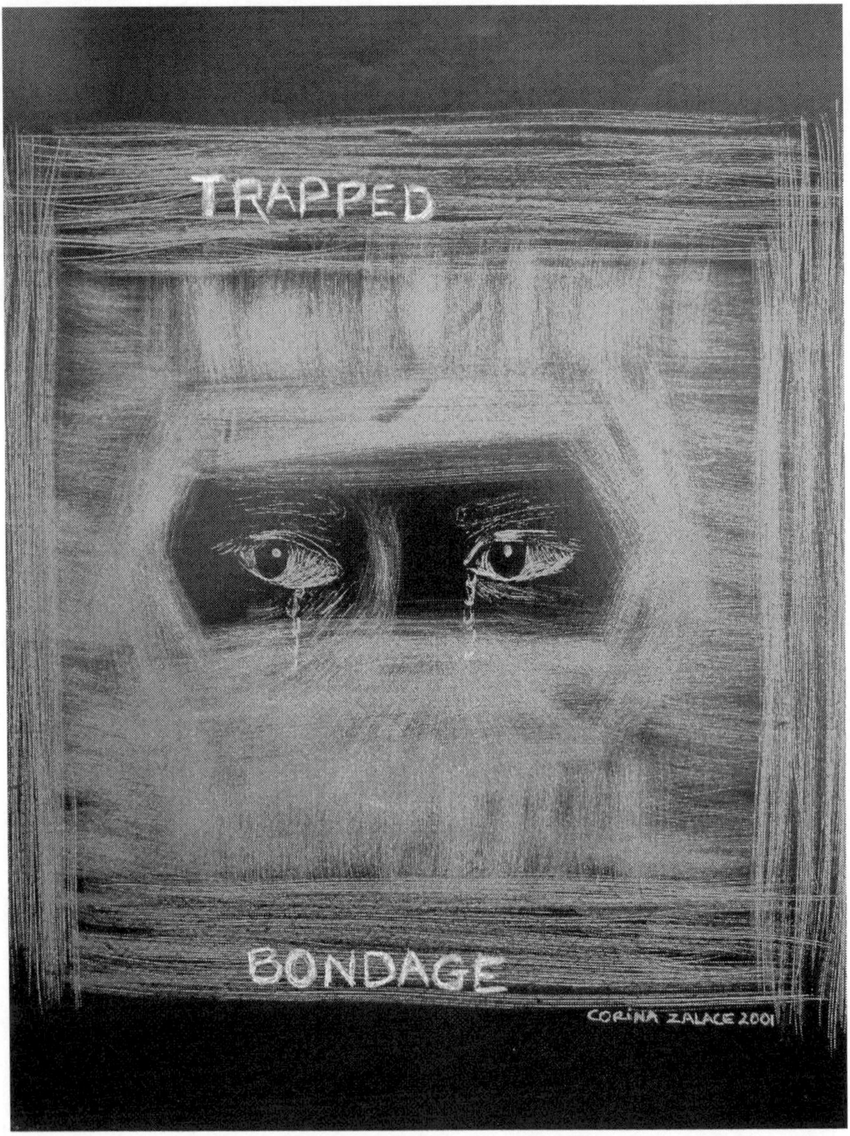
TRAPPED
BONDAGE
CORINA ZALACE 2001

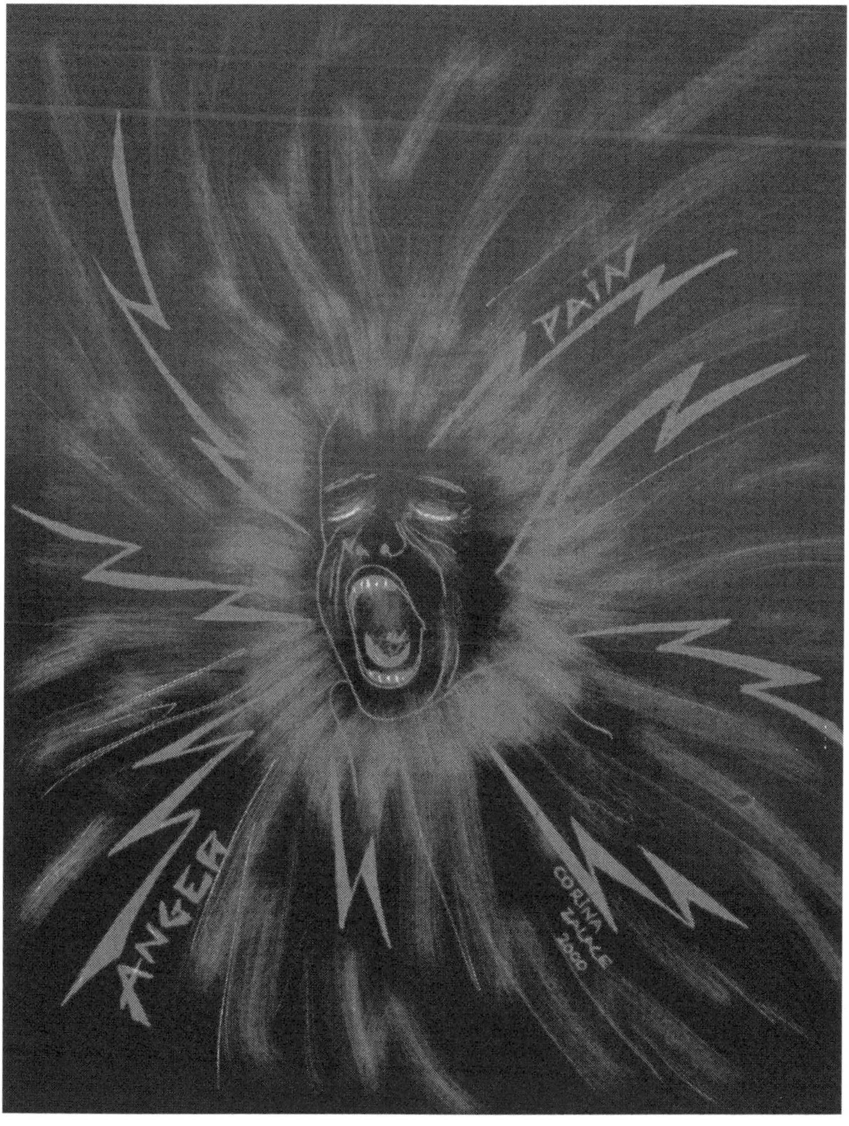
PAIN
ANGER
CORINA
2000

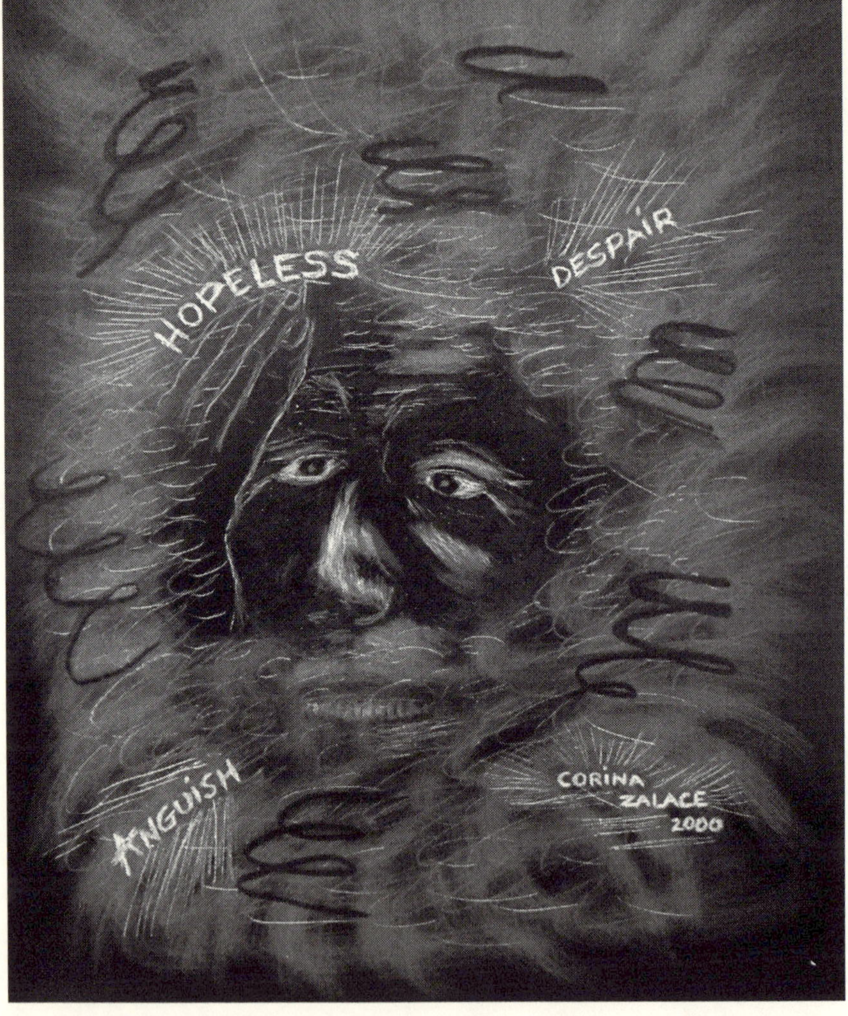
HOPELESS
DESPAIR
ANGUISH
CORINA
ZALACE
2000

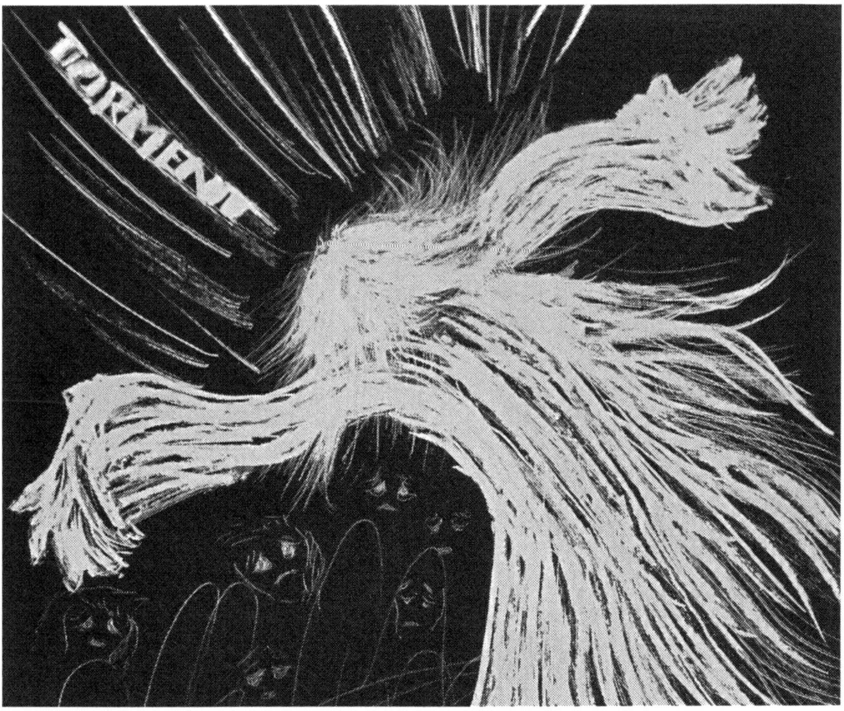
TORMENT

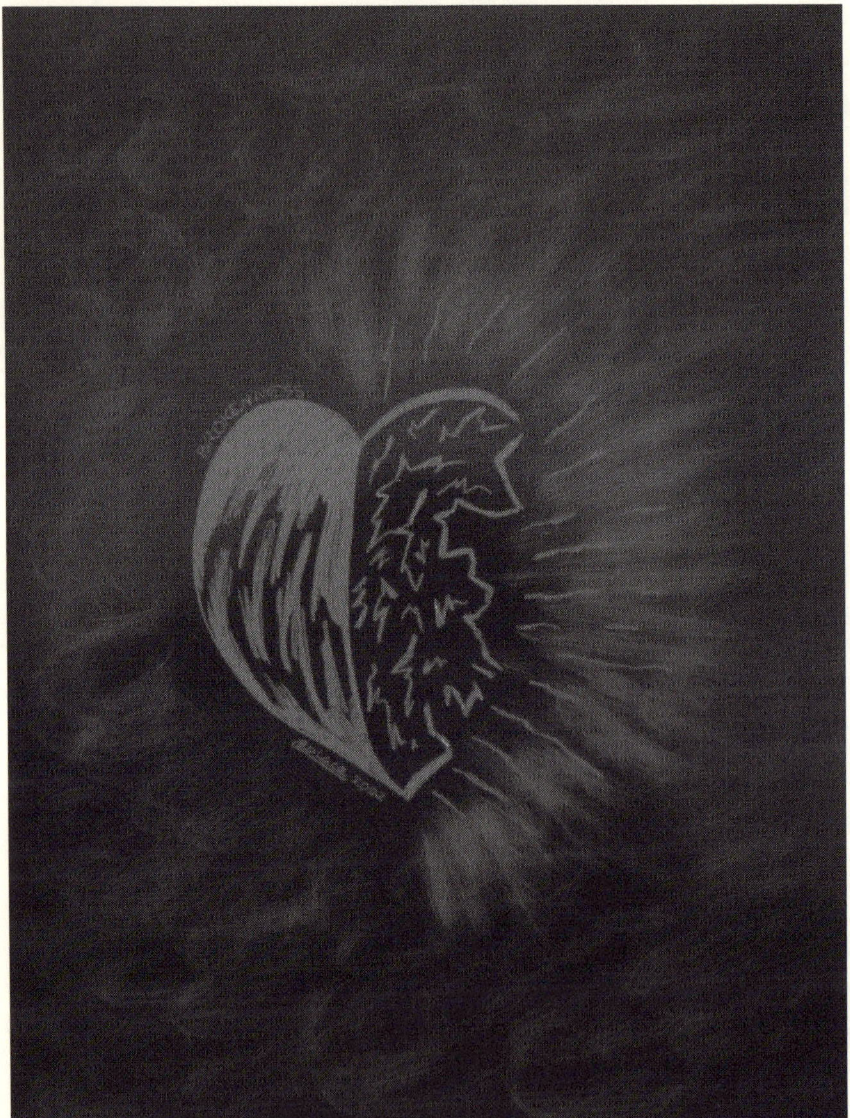

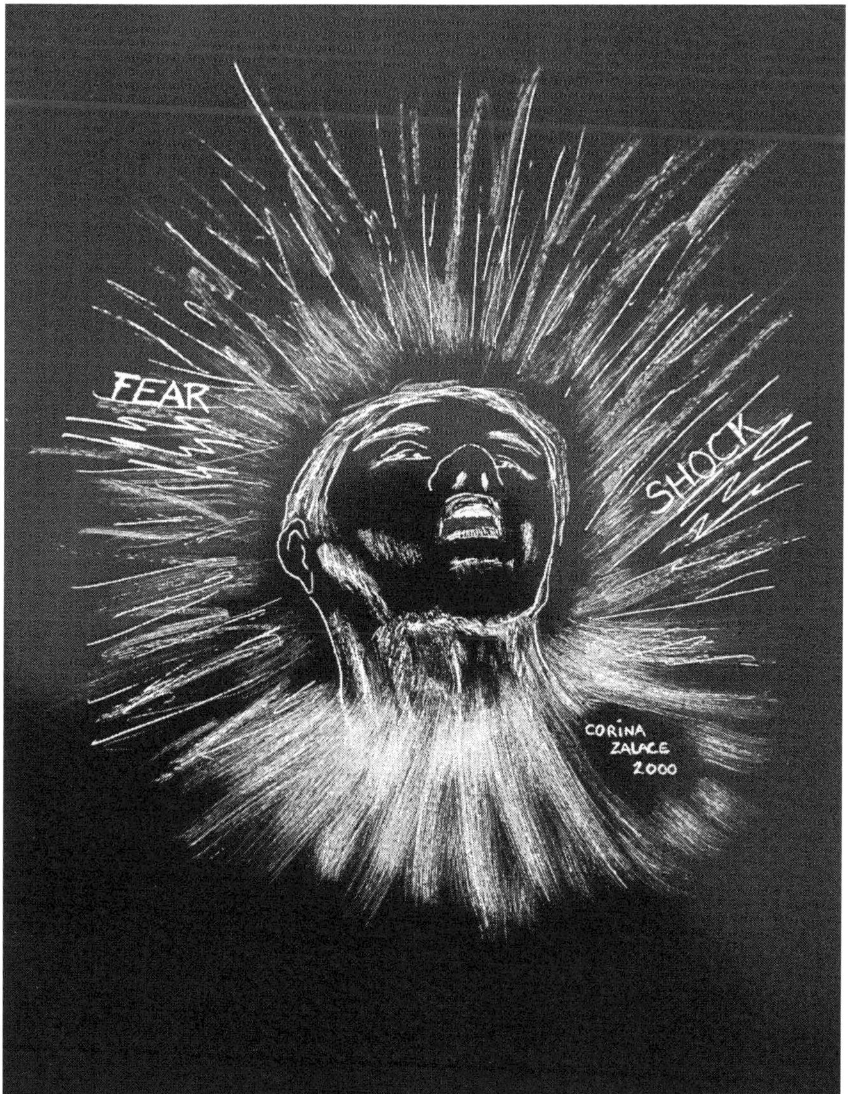
FEAR
SHOCK
CORINA
ZALACE
2000

If Only . . .

How often do we say:
"If only I had this or that,
I'd be so happy
Instead of feeling flat"?

"If only" statements are
Illusion lies that say:
"I'd be happy if and when . . ."
But really just lead us astray.

I have lived my life
Most of the time this way;
Wishing for escape routes
By desiring the "if only" way.

It is very hard to live
A full life in this dream;
For that is all it is:
A dream void of self-esteem.

A theme or goal I must
Accomplish in my life;
But living the "if only"
Only helped me avoid strife.

I was not accepting
God's life for me,
So I got stuck in a rut
Feeling miserable, not free.

Since I accepted reality
And not the "if only" way,
I have been so much happier
And thankful for every day!

For God has very carefully
Planned for me to thrive,
And choosing to live His way
Makes me more alive!

Habakkuk 3: 17 – 18

Even though the fig trees have no blossoms
And there are no grapes on the vine;
Even though the olive crop fails
And the fields lie empty and barren;
Even though the flocks die in the fields
And the cattle barns are empty;
YET, I will rejoice in the Lord!
I WILL be joyful in the God of my salvation,
For He is my Strength!

When all goes well
With us every single day,
It's easy to be happy
As success leads our way.

We tend not to grumble
About even petty things,
Because every thing's fine,
In our life without sufferings.

We enjoy each other
And the things we do.
Life is so good then, and each day
New pleasures we pursue.

It's easy to praise God
During times like these
When we feel so good,
Happy and at ease.

But, what if pain
Of any type
Invades our life,
Causing us to gripe?

A death, a divorce,
Chronic physical pain;
Mental agony, depression,
Things that our spirit drain.

Cancer, diseases
And other maladies;
Life can seem so cruel,
Overwhelmed with tragedies.

Betrayal by a friend
Can be so painful
Making our emotions
Harsh and baleful.

The question is:
How will we react
When all goes wrong,
Everything we do attacked?

Will we cry?
Will we scream?
Will we become bitter
Or hide away and dream.

Will we curse God
And shake our fist?
Blaming Him for all
The failures on our list?

Yes, let it out,
God can take it all,
For in the end
Our goal is to stand, not fall.

So, will we choose
To rejoice in Him?
Blessing and praising,
Making our lives a hymn?

No matter what trials
We go through in life,
God is focused on
Our attitude through strife.

Nothing in our life
Will God allow to be in vain,
Turning bad things to good
For His glorifying gain.

The Transformation

Twelve disciples
Were called by Him
To walk each day
Along a path often grim.

Wherever He went
They were at His side.
He taught them much;
They learned in Him to abide.

One day He chose
Three of His clan
To go up the mountain;
It was part of His plan.

So from the lush valley
They began to ascend.
Up the rugged path
To the summit they did wend.

Jesus did not meet them
At the top of the mound.
He walked up with them
Very willingly, they found.

Reaching the top,
Jesus became transformed.
Never had they seen Him
Appear so wonderfully formed.

Light surrounded Him;
Moses and Elijah stood near.
It truly was ecstasy;
All wanted to remain in His sphere.

It felt like heaven,
So wonderfully pure.
A miracle moment
They hoped would endure.

Just like the disciples,
Jesus calls each of us
To walk with Him
And abide in all He does.

But the path to the summit
Is rugged and steep.
Many steps are painful,
Many tears we must weep.

Many find His path
Too difficult to walk.
They appear to follow God,
But it's just a lot of talk.

Only those who are willing
To walk where Christ will lead,
Shall behold His transformation
And with His standards accede.

Healing From My Secret

I see three big gates,
Rusty from age,
Towering before me,
Like the side of a cage.

Looking through the gates,
I see a large box
Wrapped in brown paper,
Standing massive like an ox.

I want to run away
From what I must face,
And get away from
This terrible place.

But then I feel Jesus
Standing beside me.
He completely understands
What I must dare to see.

He stretches out
His hand to me.
And in His palm
Three large keys I see.

Keys made of gold
And beautifully they shine.
He tells me to take them
But I pull back and whine.

I am frightened of
What I will find,
For I Know I need to open
The large box over which I whined.

The golden keys unlock
Every towering gate.
And once unlocked I must face
That which I really hate.

But Jesus assures me,
That what is in the box
Is precious and beautiful,
Unlike my menacing ox.

I take a big risk
By taking the three keys.
Now I must decide
How to use these scary keys.

Must I unlock
Each gate in turn,
Or open all three
And chance my world won't burn?

I look at Jesus
For direction on this,
For I don't want to
Do something amiss

I ask Him this question:
"Why are the keys gold
When the gates are rusty
And so very old?"

He answers me gently,
"My child, why would I
Give you old rusty keys if
For the gold ones I chose to die?"

I then ask Him
"Why are there three?
I don't understand.
Why three is important to me."

Again He replied gently
"The gates and keys are three,
For the three memories of sexual
Abuse from which you still try to flee."

It begins to make sense,
For at age seven
I was sexually abused
And my spirit was left broken.

A family servant had lured me
Away from our home, then I was raped.
And out in a field he did
Things that my whole life reshaped.

"So what do I do now
My dear Savior and Lord?
I want to be set free
From memories I abhorred.

"They have affected me
In so many ways
And in my relationships
They affect me every day."

Jesus then shows me that
The gates each have a name:
Disgust, Filth, Shame.
Names causing me great pain.

He looks at me
And motions for me
To come hold his hand,
So in my heart I can be free.

He then leads me
To each rusty gate.
First I open "Disgust,"
And then I stand and wait.

To my surprise and delight
I see "Disgust" quickly leave,
Making me feel much lighter
Than I could ever believe.

Now I'm excited
To open the next gate.
As I turn the key
"Filth" screams and falls prostrate.

OK . . . now it's "Shames" turn,
And it flees aghast;
Now I must face the brown box
That so twisted and controlled my past.

The brown paper that
Enfolds the box
Is called "reluctance,"
And it my growing resolve mocks.

Holding Jesus' hand
I approach the box slowly.
I don't want to open it.
It makes me want to flee.

Jesus assures me
There's a treasure inside.
Will I trust Him in this
And not feel petrified?

After some time
I finally decide
To open the box
And take a peek inside.

I open it very slowly,
With trembling and fear,
For I am still burdened
With memories full of tears.

Still holding Jesus' hand
I look for answers to my life inside.
And what I found:
A peace that would abide.

Peace seems such a simple thing, but
A peace that passes understanding
Is far beyond mankind's grasp
Without Christ's gentle blessing.

His peace just flows
Around and through me.
"Reluctance" is gone
And inside I feel free.

Jesus then speaks:
"From now on stay
Closely to my side,
And from Me do not stray."

"All things of me
Are beautiful and holy.
We will take each step together
So depend upon me wholly."

I feel so different,
Wonderful and light
Jesus will guide me
As in Him there is no sleight.

He and I will explore
My new found world
Together hand in hand.
With Him there is no netherworld.

Thank you so much Jesus,
For setting me free
From my agonizing past . . .
Now just a distant memory.

Epilogue

II Samuel 22, Verses 1-4
    When the Lord saved David from Saul and his other enemies, David sang this song to the Lord:

    The Lord is my protector;
    He is my strong fortress.
    My God is my protection,
    And with Him I am safe.

    He protects me like a shield;
    He defends me and keeps me safe.
    He is my savior;
    He protects me and saves me

    From violence.
    I call to the Lord,
    And he saves me from my enemies.
    Praise the Lord!

II Samuel 22, Verses 17-21
    The Lord reached down from
    Above and took hold of me;
    He pulled me out of the deep
    waters.

    He rescued me from my
    Powerful enemies.
    And from all those who hate
    Me—
    They were too strong for me.
    When I was in trouble they
    Attacked me,

But the Lord protected me.
He helped me out of danger;
He saved me because he was
   Pleased with me.

The Lord rewards me because
   I do what is right;
He blesses me because I am
   Innocent.

Good News Bible
©1976

Postscript

Life is like art. In art, black is a very necessary color to give fullness, depth and contrast to a painting. Without it, the painting looks flat and dull.

The same is true in life: The dark times that we so hate allow God to make the most significant changes in us. These are times of self-reflection, slowing down, and seeking God for answers and healing. Eventually, each of us will have walked through our personal valley with Jesus to reach the mountaintop of joy, peace and strength we are meant to achieve. Jesus had to endure a 40-day wilderness experience and then the Gethsemane experience in obedience to His Father. So let us look to Jesus continually for guidance and direction, for only with Him can we get true healing, whether He uses doctors, therapists or other professionals. Never be ashamed to use these gifted people God has given wisdom and understanding to help others. Most of my healing has occurred through God using people in my life. Remember, "No man is an island . . ."

No Man Is An Island

No man is an island,
Entire of itself.
Each is a piece of the continent,
A part of the main.

If a clod be washed away by the sea,
Europe is the less.
As well as if a promontory were.
As well as if a manor of thine own

Or of thine friend's were.
Each man's death diminishes me,
For I am involved in mankind.

Therefore, send not to know
For whom the bell tolls,
It tolls for thee.

John Donne

An Abbreviated List Of Works By Corina Zalace

Scientific illustrations in the Journal of Mammalogy
Scientific illustrations in the Journal of Paleontology
Scientific illustrations in the Journal of Herpetology

Illustrations in books:
Mammals of North-Central Texas
The Flowering Dates of Florida's Wildflowers

Illustrated and written works:
My Life As A Seed:
Making Sense Out Of Darkness

The Story Of Cate:
Our Transformation

Book edited by Stanley Zalace

Edwards Brothers Malloy
Oxnard, CA USA
July 15, 2014